Wilde

Wayfinding

Wilderness Wayfinding

How to Survive in the Wilderness As You Travel

Bob Newman

Illustrations by Susan Newman

PALADIN PRESS
BOULDER, COLORADO

For my father,
William R. Newman,
for pointing the way and letting go

Wilderness Wayfinding:
How to Survive in the Wilderness As You Travel
by Bob Newman

Illustrations by Susan Newman.

CONTENTS

1   Introduction

7   Chapter One
     The Mystery of the Map

27   Chapter Two
     Comprehending the Compass

33   Chapter Three
     Principles of Map and Compass Work

43   Chapter Four
     Putting It All Together

55   Chapter Five
     Tricks of the Trade

71   Chapter Six
     The Environment Angle

79   Chapter Seven
     Primitive Means

89   Chapter Eight
     Survival and the Wayfinder

145 Chapter Nine
     Weather or Not

153 Chapter Ten
     The Great Alone

ACKNOWLEDGMENTS

I would be remiss to not first thank my father, William R. Newman, for taking me into the woods and onto the waters where I first began to learn about nature. He gave me my first compass, lent me a few words of advice, and turned me loose in the Maine woods. I was 10 years old and never looked back.

Some of my best times out in the boonies were in the company of Chief Kevin Garner of the Royal Navy, who I was fortunate to hook up with while we were wilderness survival instructors at the U.S. Navy Survival School in Redington, Maine. Kevin's vast knowledge of wayfinding opened my eyes to a trick or two from time to time, and his classic British calm under pressure was a thing to behold.

My two boyhood hunting partners, John Shesler and Steve ("Skeet") King, of Thomaston, Maine, rewarded me with their company and kept me laughing. I owe them both.

Zip, my trusting black Labrador retriever who passed on many years ago on the shores of the pond where he chased geese and ducks, brought me back when my wayfinding came up a little lacking. I'll meet you in the woods, boy.

And finally, my wife Susan's encouragement was, as always, the one thing that kept me plodding along, despite a war, countless extended trips away from hearth and home to distant lands, and innumerable nights spent under the stars. You are my compass, Suzy.

INTRODUCTION

Wha is the allure we feel when we hear the word "wilderness"? Why do most of us picture only a forested mountain range with snow-capped peaks, icy crystalline streams, and endless roadless tracts that are home to moose, raptors, mountain lion, beaver, and bear, when wilderness is also the vast expanses of the Gobi Desert, the shocking aloneness of the Siberian tundra, the screeching jungles of Mindoro, the shimmering waves of the South American pampas, and the merciless void of the Australian Outback? Why do we feel that almost hidden tinge of fear when we see ourselves lost and alone in one of these remarkable environments? Our thoughts turn to the rigors of survival, and we envision a gruesome, lonely demise far from the comforts we have all become so accustomed to. Civilization is like that. It makes us complacent and trusting, with no nightmares about life in what the late poet Robert W. Service called "The Great Alone," until one day when we suddenly find ourselves thrust into a life or death struggle with the wilderness and its overseer, nature.

How can this allure coexist with trepidation? I believe it is our past beckoning to us from a distant yesteryear, calling us back to hardier days filled with toil, adventure,

The first explorers in the Yosemite valley had to have sharp wayfinding skills.

and earnest travail in the heart of an emerald and azure forest teeming with life. In the last century man could be found exploring North America (among countless other places) with little more than a pack horse or two, a well-chosen cache of supplies, a rifle, and his wits. He knew the secrets of the land and understood precisely how to survive and travel the wilderness without a compass, topographic map, or Global Positioning System (GPS) terminal attached to his rawhide belt. He knew that moss doesn't grow only on the north side of trees and rocks. He could glance at the stars to determine in what direction he was traveling. He understood that the low ground between two hills or mountains (a saddle) often affords comparatively easy passage to the regions beyond. And he could look at vegetation from miles away and know whether or not he should detour around a particular terrain feature. Man was an integral part of nature, not wanting to remove himself from it, but rather to become more deeply immersed in its mysterious ways so that he would survive to see the dawn.

In this modern world where we now find ourselves, it is easy to depend on high-tech means to get us from here to there. I am not about to belittle these navigational wonders, devices such as the GPS currently in use with U.S. Armed Forces, however, because they are truly remarkable and extremely useful. GPS got us through the battles of the Gulf War, and I suspect we would have had a little more difficulty over there had we not had this system. We had heard about this gadget before it arrived, having read of its capabilities in various magazines, reports, and papers. But when we got it we were still surprised and more than a little skeptical. It was given to us new in the box and came with a battery and directions that claimed it would not only tell us exactly where we were, but would even tell us how to get to where we were going by informing us when we had to turn left or right, how far we had traveled, how far we still had to go, and so on.

But what was more astonishing than all these claims, and its incredibly small size, was the fact that it actually did everything it said it would do. Everything. The great foreboding mystery of desert navigation had just been solved in a neat, trim little olive drab package that was user friendly and simple.

Still, we had some navigation debacles in that ancient desert that proved beyond a doubt that technology will never solve all our problems and won't always be there when we need it most.

One evening one of my marines left his hooch (living) hole and began walking toward his fighting hole, a distance of no more than 25 yards, which he had walked dozens of times in the past week or so. He never made it, having walked straight past his fighting hole and out into the desert toward the Iraqi lines.

There was no moon, but some stars were visible. He had no compass but should still have known enough to take a quick bearing on the stars and get himself moving in the right direction. But he didn't. Hours later he miraculously stumbled into a marine artillery unit to our north, which was the last friendly unit between us and the Iraqis. As the dawn crept across the desert morning, he saw his unit a few miles distant and came home with his tail tucked firmly between his legs.

This little story proves beyond a doubt that wilderness navigation is still an essential skill to many people in a variety of walks of life: the snowmobiler caught in a blizzard deep in the woods whose machine breaks down at the worst possible moment, the game warden who must trek into the wilds to find a lost hiker, the hunter who pursues a wounded elk far into the backcountry, and the airplane crash survivor who must find his way back to civilization. All must know how to navigate in the wilderness, but more importantly, they must know how to wayfind.

Don't confuse wayfinding with navigation. Navigation is finding your way by using one or a series of azimuths or bearings, which are linear paths referenced by degrees on a compass. Wayfinding is a broader term that deals with finding your way through a wilderness or backwoods area by using natural routes—routes that will almost certainly not be linear. It also encompasses primitive means of position determination (self-location), and relates to wilderness travel on a broader scale.

This book will teach you, regardless of your background, how to find your way in any terrain under almost any conditions. You will learn how to use terrain to assist you in traveling, determine direction by the stars, use the sun and moon as compasses, tell how far you have traveled, decipher the mysteries of a topographic map, associate any terrain feature you see on your map with what you see on the Earth's surface before you, plot bearings and back-bearings, fix the position of a feature you can see on the map, safely and effectively detour around potential danger areas, and much, much more. You will even learn how to survive in the wilderness as you travel. This is the first book to cover it all.

So come along and join me in the wilderness.

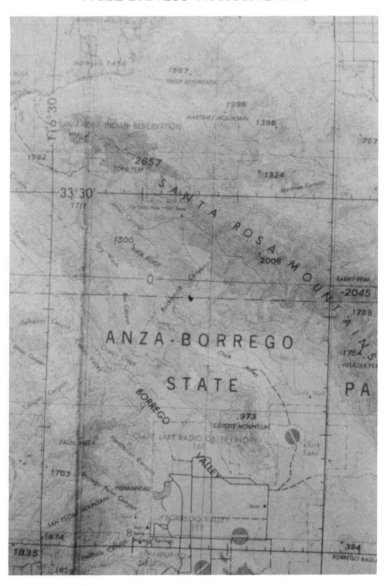

This topo map of the Anza Borrego Desert shows numerous terrain features.

CHAPTER ONE

THE MYSTERY OF THE MAP

There are numerous maps available to us nowadays. There are political maps, which are specialized to deal with town and city boundaries. Planimetric maps show no measurable terrain relief indicators and depict horizontal positions of certain features. Your standard city map doesn't show relief but does show roads, buildings, and other major features both man-made and natural, such as a pond in a park. Charts are maps dealing primarily with water. There are others, too, but the kind of map we will concern ourselves with in this chapter is the topographic map.

Before we go into a detailed discussion of topographic maps, you should first know certain facts about "topo" maps in general.

Just what is a topo map? Simply stated, it is a two-dimensional representation of a selected portion of the Earth's surface that is drawn to a particular scale and placed on paper of some kind, and shows relief and elevation via contour lines. Though it is not a photograph, a topographic map can be thought of as a picture of sorts. If you were to take a photograph of a section of the Earth's surface by shooting straight down from a hot air balloon hovering several thousand feet in the air on a clear day, the photo would reveal many features and facts about the land below. You could see farms and power lines, brooks and fields, woods and dams. You could also see terrain features such as mountains, hills, valleys, and knolls. Even the subtle features such as small rises in the lay of the land could be made out if you knew what to look for in the picture. But a topo map makes it easy for you by using those brownish, squiggly lines known as contour lines. Those contour lines, once you understand how they work and what they mean, will tell you how steep a certain piece of terrain is (the slope) and the elevation at a certain spot. Contour lines are neither mysterious nor confusing.

The scale of the map is important. Having a topo map with an inconvenient scale (too small or too large) is annoying and frustrating, so be sure to buy the one that best suits your needs. Scale actually refers to the degree of reduction and is represented as a fraction—1:25,000 or 1:100,000, for instance. This degree of reduction refers to how much smaller the topographic map is than the region it depicts. So, if I have a 1:50,000 (read as one to fifty-thousand) scale topo map, I know that 1 inch of distance on the map itself equals 50,000 inches on the ground (not accounting for relief). Do not confuse the bar scales in the map's margin with the scale of the map; the bar scales have a completely different use and are discussed later in this chapter.

You can find the scale of the map in the map's margin along with a great deal of other essential information (as well as some information that you may never need). Before you can effectively use a map to get around, you need to know what this marginal information means and how to put it to good use.

THE LEGEND

Your topographic map's legend shows and explains the various symbols used. Never assume that the symbols on one topographic map are precisely the same as those on another. They may be different.

The legend tells you a great deal about what you are seeing on the map. It shows you how buildings, windmills, rapids, orchards, levees, proposed roads, tunnel

BENCH MARK, MONUMENTED	BM ×123
BENCH MARK, NONMONUMENTED	×321
CHURCH; SCHOOL	
BUILDINGS/STRUCTURES	
TANKS; LOCATED OBJECTS	
OPEN PIT MINE/QUARRY	
HORIZONTAL CONTROL STATION	

Legend Symbols (a)

entrances, intermittent lakes, canals with locks, and untold other features are depicted. If you fail to pay close attention to these symbols, you could find yourself in a situation you could have avoided and really don't want to have to deal with. A classic example of this is the desert

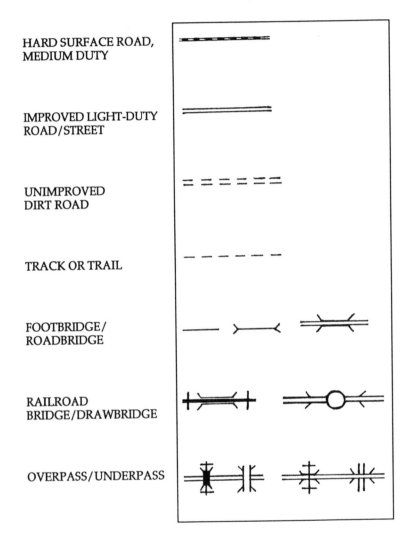

Legend Symbols (b)

THE MYSTERY OF THE MAP

mule deer hunter who becomes lost. After using up all his water, he scans his map for the umpteenth time and sees a

RAILROAD, SINGLE & DOUBLE TRACK	
VINEYARD	
ORCHARD	
POWER TRANSMISSION LINE	
MARSH OR SWAMP	
CEMETERY	
INTERMITTENT LAKE/STREAM	

Legend Symbols (c)

lake only nine miles away. A small lake, but a lake never-theless. He manages to get his bearings and makes off toward the distant lake.

Upon arrival, after a long and grueling trek, he discovers that the lake is bone dry. Not believing what he is seeing in front of him, he breaks out the map again and takes another look. Then he sees where he went wrong. This is the lake all right, but he failed to note that the lake is depicted as intermittent (seasonal) on the map. He thought those dashes along the lake's perimeter on the map represented some sort of fence a rancher had erected. Big mistake, eh? Might just be his last, too.

Never glance at the legend. Study it.

SHEET NAME

The sheet name is simply the name of the map and is usually arrived at by determining the major geographic or cultural (man-made) feature shown on the map. You will normally find the sheet name at the top center of the topo map and also in the lower right-hand corner. It is much easier to find the exact map you are looking for if you know the sheet name.

SHEET NUMBER

The sheet number is part of a reference system used to determine what map adjoins another. It is often found in the upper right-hand margin of the topographic map.

SERIES NAME

Topographic maps are frequently made in series because a particular geographic region can't be covered all on one map. This information is most often located in the upper left-hand corner or thereabouts. The map scale is found here, too.

DECLINATION DIAGRAM

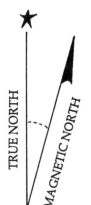

This little jewel will be discussed in great detail later on, but you can find the declination diagram somewhere along the lower margin.

Declination Diagram

BAR SCALES

Bar scales are used to measure distance on the map and are normally found in the lower margin. They show meters, yards, and statute/nautical miles.

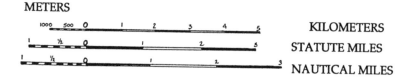

Bar Scales

PROTRACTOR SCALE

The better topographic maps have this scale, which is used with your compass to orient the map to true north. When it is placed on a map it usually shows up along the upper margin.

ELEVATION GUIDE

Large scale maps (normally considered to be maps at a scale of 1:75,000 or greater) sometimes have an elevation guide, which is simply a tiny diagram in the lower right-hand margin that depicts primary drainage features such as major rivers, important mountain ranges, spot elevations, and so on.

SERIES NUMBER

The series number is found in two places in the map's margin (upper right-hand corner and lower left-hand corner). It is used for ordering information.

EDITION NUMBER

This reference system has to do with the topographic map's age in comparison to other maps of the same region. The higher the number the more recently the map was constructed. However, keep in mind that the very second a map is printed, it is out of date. We'll discuss this in more detail later.

HORIZONTAL DATUM NOTE

This is one of the pieces of information found in the margin that you may never need, but which cartographers may. All it is is a system that refers to the horizontal control station network that deals with every mapped feature's horizontal position on the map. It is in the lower margin, centered.

VERTICAL DATUM NOTE

The same thing as the horizontal datum note, but this note also covers elevation and contour. It is found with the horizontal datum note.

CONTOUR INTERVAL

Very important. This tells you what the difference in elevation is between contour lines. It can vary radically from map to map. It is found in the lower center margin.

COVERAGE DIAGRAM

A coverage diagram tells you what system was used to acquire the information used to compile the map, how good the sources are considered to be, and the dates of photos used. It is most often found in the right-hand or lower margin.

STOCK NUMBER IDENTIFICATION

If your topo is of a military nature, it will have a stock number identification that uses the series and sheet numbers and maybe the edition number, too.

CREDIT NOTE

Similar to the coverage diagram, the credit note (located in the lower left-hand margin) tells you how the map was prepared, the date it was printed, and what methods were used in compilation.

ADJOINING SHEETS DIAGRAM

A schematic showing rectangles adjoining one another, which are adjoining maps, and their sheet numbers.

GRID REFERENCE BOX

Used mostly by cartographers, this is used to construct a grid reference.

USER'S NOTE

This is a message to the map user requesting that he notify the agency that created the map of any changes that need to be made.

GRID NOTE

This deals with what grid system was used, grid value omissions, and grid line intervals. It is usually located in the lower center margin.

UNIT IMPRINT

Tells the topographic map user who made the map and the date it was printed. Again, remember that a map is out of date as soon as it is printed, and keep in mind that this date does not reflect the date the information was gathered, but rather the date the data was all put together as a map and printed.

PROJECTION NOTE

This reassures the user that shapes shown on the map, both geographic and cultural are true, measured angles are nearly precise, and the scale is true everywhere on the map. It is in the lower margin.

BOUNDARIES INDEX

Another map miniature, this one details political boundaries such as town lines, county lines, parish lines, et al.

From time to time additional marginal information may show up. If you have a question as to what a particular diagram means, write the map's maker.

MAP COLORS AND WHAT THEY MEAN

Topo maps use various colors to indicate what certain features are. There are five primary map colors, but sometimes others show up.

In any case, any unusual colors will be explained in the margin. The primary colors are blue, black, red, green, and brown.

Brown—contour lines and other relief features are shown in brown or brownish red.

Blue—all water features including perennial and intermittent creeks, brooks, streams, rivers, lakes, and ponds. Oceans and seas also come out blue, as you might expect. Swamps appear blue and green, with water being blue and the green being vegetation around or in the water.

Black—all man-made (cultural) features such as water tanks, churches, bridges, wrecks (ships and boats), pipelines, and so on are shown in black.

Red—main roadways, urban areas, and certain "special" features are shown in red. Note that on some topo maps urban areas are shown in yellow.

Green—all vegetation, whether it is wild or cultivated, is shown in green. The topographic map symbols chart shows you what the different symbols within a green area are. Sometimes shading is used to depict relative thickness of vegetation; the darker the shading, the thicker the vegetation.

CONTOUR LINES: A VITAL FACTOR

Contour, which means form, refers to the lay of the land when dealing with wayfinding, navigation, and topographic maps. Contour lines do not exist in nature; they are imaginary. The only place I know of where contour lines are found is on a topographic map. These lines show relief (the

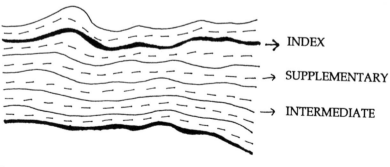

→ INDEX

→ SUPPLEMENTARY

→ INTERMEDIATE

Contour Lines

lay of the land) and elevation. Any two locations along a single contour line are at the same elevation, regardless of how radically the surrounding terrain appears to deviate between the two points. Don't forget that.

Contour lines tell you more important information about a piece of land than any other map symbol. They show you not only the big picture, but the subtle details of a region, too. Contour lines show hills, knolls, depressions, fingers, saddles, ridges, ranges, mountains, valleys, draws, eskers, and every other terrain feature you can think of. The trick, however, is to be able to tell the difference between all of these and then use that knowledge to guide you to wherever it is you are heading.

Actually, it is no trick at all, merely another learned skill, just like driving a car, water-skiing, fly-tying, walking, and speaking a foreign language. Deciphering the intricacies of a topo map's contour lines is easy.

Before we get into a detailed description of what different terrain features look like on a topographic map, keep one important rule in mind: the closer the contour lines are, the greater the slope. Barely separated contour lines show a steep slope; widely spaced contour lines mean a gentle slope. Also, always note the contour interval in the center lower margin. Contour interval often differs greatly from map to map, especially maps of different scales. One map may have a contour interval of 20 feet, while another may have a contour interval of 20 meters. That is a tremendous difference!

HILLS

Hills are depicted by contour lines forming a roughly circular shape. Don't think that a hill must appear perfectly circular. It doesn't, and they rarely do. For a hill to form a perfectly circular shape on a topo map it would necessarily have to be perfectly conical in shape on the ground. No dimples, wrinkles, divots, or any other flaw could be present. This is highly unusual, to say the least. Knolls appear as hills that are closer to being perfectly round but are generally smaller than hills.

Hill

MOUNTAINS

Mountains, I suppose, are giant hills. Where we draw the line between a mountain and a hill, I have no idea. After all, a mountain in Georgia would be considered a barely discernable rise in the land to my friend Norm Campbell in Cordova, Alaska. By the same token, a mountain in Cordova, Alaska, wouldn't qualify as such to a Sherpa guide in Nepal's Himalayas. So mountains are a relative term. However, for our purposes let's consider a mountain to be land mass whose elevation exceeds 3,000 feet and which clearly emanates from much lower terrain surrounding it.

Contour lines depict mountains in a similar manner as hills, but they are often shown with much greater slopes and are frequently found in ranges, that is, a line or group of mountains forming a massive picket or gathering of summits. Some mountains, though, crop up from the Earth's surface all by their lonesome.

You can determine the elevation of a mountain's summit (and the top of a hill, too) by determining what the value of the highest contour line is and then adding one-half of the contour interval to that figure. Many summits (and hilltops), however, have the precise elevation indicated thereon. They may also have a bench mark indicator there, which is shown on a topo map as the letters BM followed by the small letter X, and then the elevation. If no benchmark has been placed on that spot, the BM will be deleted. (A benchmark is most often a steel or iron plate sunk and anchored into the ground at a certain spot by the U.S. Geological Survey, denoting elevation, date, and so on.)

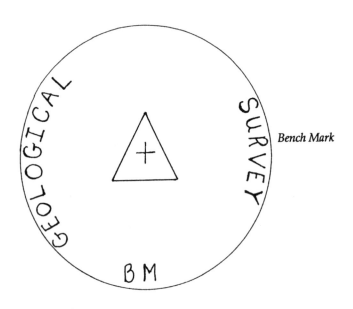

Bench Mark

There are two types of mountain ridges: (1) those formed by a series of hilltops that are clearly part of the same geologic formation and (2) those formed as a result of two opposing slopes meeting one another (known as a knife edge).

The former shows roughly circular-shaped contour lines with the hilltops being separated by areas of lesser elevation and usually a gentler slope, which are known as saddles. The latter is usually depicted with contour lines that reflect fairly severe slope and which run up close to each other at the top of the ridge.

THE MYSTERY OF THE MAP

SADDLES

Saddles, the lower land between two hills, are concave shapes formed by contour lines. Some are broad, others less so.

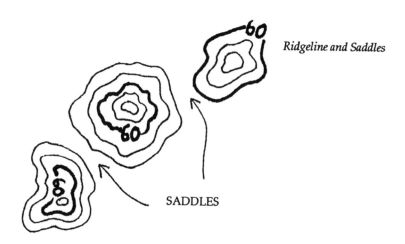

Ridgeline and Saddles

SADDLES

FINGERS

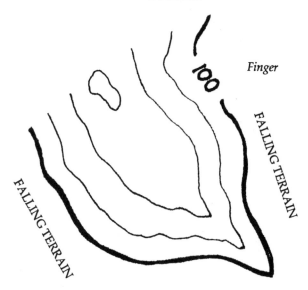

Finger

FALLING TERRAIN

FALLING TERRAIN

A finger can be likened to a ridge of sorts that runs down off a hill or mountain. It is shown by contour lines on a topographic map which form V's or U's that open uphill.

DRAWS

Draws are the inverse of fingers. They are shown as V's and U's that open uphill and are found between two fingers or one finger and an opposing slope.

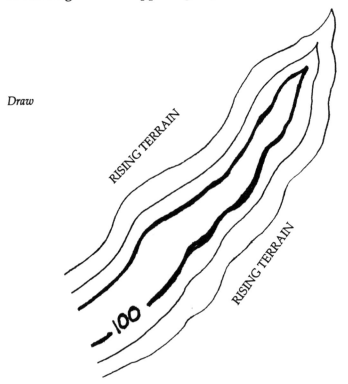

Draw

RISING TERRAIN

RISING TERRAIN

100

DEPRESSIONS

Natural depressions such as limestone sinkholes are depicted as roughly circular shapes, like a hill, but have tick marks running perpendicular to the contour lines into the depression.

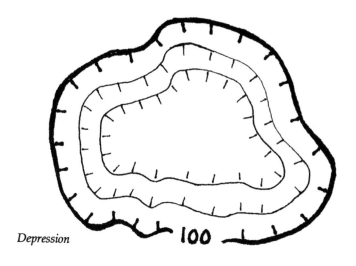

Depression

VALLEYS

Valleys are elongated lowlands between two ranges or ridges. The contour lines reflect this by showing minimal slope between the two ranges or ridges. A valley frequently has a stream or river running through it.

CUTS AND FILLS

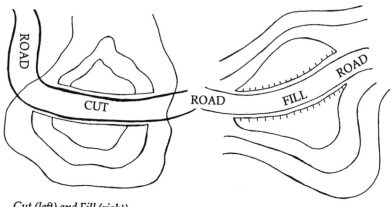

Cut (left) and Fill (right)

A cut is just that: a cut made by man through a hillside or finger. It cuts through a feature. A fill is just the opposite, it goes over (rather than through) a feature.

CLIFFS

Where two or more contour lines appear extremely close together (as when near a vertical cliff) or when the lines have tick marks pointing downhill, you have a cliff.

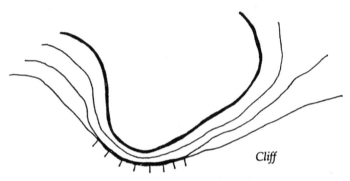

Cliff

You may have noticed that every fourth—sometimes every fifth—contour line is darker than the others. These darker lines are called index contour lines. The lighter lines between them are known as intermediate contour lines. The index lines always have their elevation written in along them at some point. Trace one with your finger and you will soon come to a number, the elevation of that line. Sometimes a topographic map will have supplementary contour lines shown as dashed brown lines between the intermediate lines. Supplementary contour lines are used to show extreme detail in relief.

Also depicted on your topo map are spot elevations. These are brown X's with a number after them. They show up at major cultural and geologic terrain features.

Well, that is the basic information you will need to at least understand a topographic map. But using that map in wayfinding is something altogether different. This practical application will be covered later.

Knowing how to move safely and effectively in extreme terrain will save you time and trouble.

CHAPTER TWO

COMPREHENDING THE COMPASS

The question has been posed of me, "If you could only have one, a map or a compass, which would you select?" I answered, "The map," because I can always tell direction but can't tell what lies beyond the next range without a map or some previously gleaned information. But this answer is too pat. Fact is, sometimes a compass would be of far more use than a map. It really depends on the situation.

Like a topographic map, a compass is a tool. Unfortunately, many people don't understand how to use a compass effectively. Oh, they know how it works, sort of, but when it comes right down to it they can barely do anything other than follow a basic north-south bearing. Being able to use a compass like a professional timber cruiser with 50 years of backwoods experience or a lifelong wilderness guide and outfitter in the Bob Marshall Wilderness will make wayfinding easier and safer. However, don't expect to walk away from this book with this kind of insight. This book—or no book for that matter—could ever replace genuine hands-on experience, but this book *will* get you onto the right track.

AN ALMOST NEW DEVICE

The name of the man (woman?) who invented the compass is uncertain, though it is widely believed that a European is due the credit for this truly monumental invention. But it wasn't a European at all. The Arabs were probably the first to use a compass of sorts to ply the waters of the Mediterranean, Red Sea, Persian Gulf, and Indian Ocean, and it appears that this technology may have been transferred to the Chinese at some point. The Arabs suspended a thin sliver of magnetite (lodestone) from a string to determine north, and therefore other directions. The Chinese thought a little differently; Chinese mariners carried out their extensive trade largely to the south and west and therefore oriented themselves that way. Chinese writings clearly indicate that they believed a sliver of magnetite gently placed on a small bed of straw floating in a bowl of water pointed south. It doesn't make any difference, really, because either direction is simply a reference from which other directions can be determined.

About 200 years before Columbus almost discovered America (come now, Norsemen were cruising the waters off Nova Scotia long before ol' Chris ever ventured onto the scene), an enterprising European redesigned the compass so that the magnetite balanced on a pivot in a protective housing. It worked very well and was soon in use on vessels of all types. The pivot compass is still used today, a fact that testifies to its usefulness.

THE PRINCIPLE

What makes a compass tick? We know that there are two kinds of north, right? True north, which refers to the North Pole, and magnetic north, which is the north a compass' north-seeking arrow seeks out. Correct? No.

There is also grid north, which refers to the grid lines on a grid map. So, technically, there are three norths, right?

COMPREHENDING THE COMPASS

No. There are five. You forgot due north and generally north. That's a joke. Well, I thought it was pretty funny.

But seriously, there are three norths: true, magnetic, and grid. Since we won't be delving much into the grid system used by the military, we'll set grid north aside and focus on true and magnetic north.

It is wrongly believed by many outdoorsmen that magnetic north is a large iron ore deposit in Canada. It is not. Magnetic north is not a place or material thing, but rather a region in the Queen Elizabeth Islands, east of Victoria Island and west of Baffin Island above the Arctic Circle. And get this: it moves. Yes, it moves, shifts. How is this possible?

Magnetic north is the region where the Earth's magnetic lines of force come together. The Earth's magnetic field is variable to some degree, which accounts for magnetic north being able to shift position in a gradual, though continual manner. This is why the U.S. Geologic Survey and the U.S. Coast and Geodetic Survey publish the variations as they occur and are detected. What is happening on the surface of the sun, or rather what happened on the surface of the sun recently and is just now getting to the Earth, affects how greatly this variation takes place and also how often. It is variable in other words. A major and continual series of solar flares can cause the Earth's magnetic lines of force to waver. However, even the most spectacular of solar flares can't cause your compass needle to jump about.

But this brings up an important point. Your compass' north seeking arrow can be drawn to metal or electromagnetic anomalies in the area, thus throwing you off. A nearby (and unseen) iron ore deposit could attract the needle and override magnetic north. So too could a vehicle a few yards away, your belt buckle a few inches away, a telephone line several yards away, and a high-tension or power line 50 or 60 yards away. Yes, that far. Don't believe me? Get your compass out and start walking toward a major power line, stopping every few steps to let the needle settle. The closer you get to the lines, the more magnetic north will vary.

DECLINATION

Declination is simply the difference in degrees between true (polar) north and magnetic north. We'll discuss how to deal with this later.

WHAT COMPASS SHOULD YOU BUY?

There are several types of compasses and hundreds of different manufacturers worldwide. My best advice to you along these lines is to buy the one you find the most useful and dependable. However, there are some important differences in design that you should be made aware of.

For as little as a few dollars you can purchase a compass that has a north-seeking arrow, the cardinal (north, south, east, and west) and intercardinal (northeast, southeast, southwest, and northwest) points inscribed on the compass card (the rotating circular disk used on some compasses) or on the housing, and perhaps a pin with which to attach the compass to your shirt or coat. This basic compass is alright for very general use but isn't nearly as useful as other, more adaptable compasses. Wayfinding often requires precise navigational skills that can be difficult to come up with when using this type of basic compass. However, in a pinch, these no-frills units can save a life, and often have.

For a few dollars more you can buy a much better compass, one that allows you to more accurately determine bearings and deal with declination. Though this design is sometimes found with a circular housing and no rectangular base, the latter model is clearly more popular and versatile, and I recommend it. This is the compensator compass.

The compensator compass' card is fixed in the base of the housing rather than on a rotating disk. A tiny screw built into the card allows the user to dial in the declination for the area he is in. What does this mean, and why is compensating for declination so important? If you are wayfinding in the backcountry between northern Maine's St. John River and the remote Quebec village of St. Pamphile, the declination (the difference in degrees between true north and magnetic north) is currently about 20° westerly, which means that you must account for this 20° of westerly declination in order to get an accurate bearing. With a compensator compass you need not do any math to arrive at this correct figure. All you do is dial in the 20° to the east on your compass card with the tiny screw. Now you have removed this error factor and all bearings taken will now be true (unless of course the compass is being thrown off by a local anomaly). If you recall from Chapter One, you find the declination for your area on the lower margin of your topographic map. If you are east of the agonic line (an imaginary line upon which there is no declination; true north and magnetic north are one and the same), you have westerly declination and must therefore account for the difference to the east. If you are west of the agonic line, you have easterly declination and must account for the difference to the west.

Another common feature of the compensator compass with a rectangular base is a direction of travel arrow built into or onto the base. This very handy reference makes travel easier. We'll discuss this more when covering compass use.

The better compensator compasses are liquid-filled. Liquid-filled housings steady the compass' needle quickly, whereas those without this feature tend to jiggle.

This type of compass also often sports a bezel ring, which is a manually rotated ring encircling the card and north-seeking arrow that has degrees on it. It is used in conjunction with the north-seeking arrow and an alignment arrow built into the compass card—where you line up the north-seeking arrow.

Other features of this type of compass include a sighting line on the cover (if it has a cover); scales along the base graduated in inches, millimeters, and centimeters; a slope scale; a luminous direction of travel arrow that comes in handy during periods of low light or actual darkness; a damping button on those not liquid-filled; and an index line on the base of the compass for reading bearings.

Another popular compass is the lensatic or military-style compass. Some come with rectangular bases, others don't. If the north-seeking arrow is part of the compass card, it is considered lensatic or military-style. The card may also have a mil scale on the card and an adjustable magnifying lens used to read bearings when the compass is held up to the eye (this is where it gets the term "lensatic"). Almost all have covers with a wire sighting line.

Finally there is the cruiser's compass, such as the one my grandfather used 50 years or so ago while "cruising" timber plots for St. Regis in northern Maine. Also known as a forester's compass, it is most often found in such people's company. Highly accurate and versatile, it has up to three different scales and several other features that a forester needs in his or her work. The degree scale on a forester's compass is set up counterclockwise.

Those are your different types of compasses. Are there others? Sure, but they are specialty models that don't really have any bearing, so to speak, here. Which one should you buy? You tell me. However, I will tell you that you should get the one you find most useful and dependable. I have had excellent results with the Silva Ranger Type 15T, an outstanding compensator compass with a rectangular base, sighting line, luminous reference dots and direction-of-travel arrow, graduated scales on the base, alignment arrow, protective cover, slope scale, and other features. However, there are other compasses of equal quality available nowadays that you may want to consider.

CHAPTER THREE

PRINCIPLES OF MAP AND COMPASS WORK

Although both the map and compass can be used separately (and very effectively), wayfinding often finds them being used together, as a team of sorts. The wilderness wayfinder should strive to be proficient at both map and compass work. You will never reach the level of expertise you seek if you are so-so at one facet of wayfinding and astounding at another. You must be sharp at every facet. This is particularly true of using the map and compass to complement each other.

Too many outdoorsmen have an adversarial role with the map and compass. The map appears to be too detailed for them to figure out, and the compass is a mysterious, untrustworthy gadget that frequently points in the wrong direction, causing them severe aggravation and endless embarrassment. How many times have we heard, "This thing is all screwed up. I know darned well that north is this way, and this stupid compass is trying to tell me that it's that way"?

Could your compass be pointing in the wrong direction? Sure. It is possible that you are near a lodestone (magnetite deposit) or some other natural or man-made anomaly that is affecting your compass. If you think this may be the case, move. Try shooting your bearing from another spot about

The wilderness wayfinder will enjoy many memorable sights.

50 yards away. If you are still convinced that the compass is wrong, move again. Check your map. Is there something indicated on the map that tells of a local magnetic disturbance? Such entries are common! And most local anomalies that are strong enough to throw off your compass are annotated on topographic maps.

Are you holding the compass level? This is important. An unleveled compass can be off by dozens of degrees.

Is it damaged? Did you drop it onto a rock? Check it.

But the truth is, *your compass is probably right*. Unless it is obviously damaged (you can clearly see the damage), or you are facing the setting sun and your compass is insisting that you are facing due east, *believe your compass!* Accept the fact that you might be a little turned around. It happens, and it happens to every outdoorsman from time to time, even in fairly familiar terrain.

One of the most memorable times I got turned around was as a wilderness survival, or SERE (Survival-Evasion-Resistance-Escape), instructor at the Navy Survival School in Maine's Redington Pond Range. I was traveling with a group of 11 survival students from a granite bluff up a long, gradual slope toward a distant ridge line. We were running on a single bearing toward a well-defined dirt road below the ridge, a trek that would take about six hours at the pace I had selected. We hadn't been moving more than an hour when we struck a dirt road that wasn't supposed to be there. I was flabbergasted.

I didn't want the group to know that we might be lost (my marine pride simply wouldn't allow that), so I stashed them in a thicket and walked out onto the road to get my bearings. Because I couldn't see much for terrain, I couldn't triangulate to get my position. But I had been keeping a pace count that I was quite confident in, so I plotted my bearing (which I was sure we had been true to) and approximate distance traveled on the map at my feet (which I had oriented to true north). This is called dead reckoning. My figuring told me that we should still be miles short of the well-defined road we were heading for and about 500 meters above a cabin known as Winter Bravo. I didn't want to run down the road looking like a fool searching for the cabin, so I gathered up the students and we struck off again toward our original destination. (I gave them some cock-and-bull story as to why we stopped.)

A few hours later, sure enough, we came out within 10 meters of where I wanted to. As soon as the students were tucked in for the night, I high-tailed it down to Winter Bravo and sped past the cabin up the old dirt road. About 500 meters past the cabin I stopped and jumped out. There were the tracks we had left earlier in the day. I checked the map and found that the dirt road I was on wasn't on it. Point #1: Your map is out of date as soon as it is printed. Point #2: Trust your compass. I have no idea why I questioned my own advice on that autumn morning so long ago, but I did. I was doubting my compass and became confused when the dirt road I was standing on didn't appear on the map. Another factor, ego, got in the way, too. I dreaded the thought of the navy instructors (sailors!) finding out about my temporary lapse in wayfinding and knew for certain that such treacherous individuals as the irrepressible John P. Lamanna, a U.S. Navy Seabee on an instructor tour at the renowned school, and Rob Brazier, a U.S. Navy SEAL also on an instructor tour (and my arch-rival), would gleefully rub my nose in the fact that, for the briefest of moments, I was somewhat less than 100 percent sure as to my precise position on the Earth's surface. Don't let vanity get in your way. Vanity and pride will kill you if you aren't careful, my friend. That lesson taught me to put arrogance aside and deal with the facts as they present themselves.

ATTENTION TO DETAIL

Wayfinding when using a map and compass to aid you (or without a map and compass, for that matter) is largely a matter of attention to detail. You must be able to note certain facts as they appear and put this information to good use. If you can't do this, you're lost.

The first step in wilderness wayfinding, no matter what situation you are in, is getting oriented. You must not only orient yourself to your surroundings, you must also orient your map as well. You can do neither without genuine attention to detail. That narrow draw on the east side of that finger below the shallow cirque may mean a great deal to you in orienting yourself and your map. If you can't relate what you see around you in the terrain to what you see on your map, you are going to have a much more difficult time of it than necessary.

This ability to relate terrain features to their representations on the map is called terrain association. It is a skill of paramount importance to the wilderness traveler. It is also known in some military circles as terrain appreciation, though this is a misleading term that I don't use. Simply stated, terrain association is being able to tell which terrain feature is which on a topographic map.

With that in mind, you should now see how important the section in Chapter One on terrain features is, i.e., how they are depicted on a topographic map. Terrain association is impossible unless you know how each terrain feature on the ground is shown on the map.

When terrain associating, it is advisable to see the big picture rather than separate terrain features taken as such. By this I mean that you should relate them to each other. This is done by inspection.

Inspection means seeing and taking it all in. Don't look merely for prominent terrain features. Instead, observe the entire panorama before you and note the relationship between different terrain features. For instance, let's say you are standing on a slight rise at the mouth of a valley. The weather is good, and you can see for several miles. On the right you note that the ridge consists of seven summits with the tallest being the sixth summit down the ridge. You also note that the fourth summit is much lower than the others, by about 600 feet or so.

The ridge on the left is quite different. Only four summits appear, with the final summit being a tremendous peak well above all the rest. You can make out a fast-moving river about three miles down the valley that runs along the valley floor and turns abruptly to the east. What appears to be a spruce bog lines a small stream on the east side of the valley.

You spread your map out on the ground and orient it. This is done by laying it on a flat piece of ground with your compass resting on it so that the north-seeking arrow is pointing to the top of the map and is precisely aligned with the edge of the map. Now you must account for declination, unless you have dialed the declination in on your compensator compass. With the compass' straight edge or the north-seeking arrow lined up precisely with one another, turn them both *simultaneously* the number of degrees of declination needed to get them both facing toward true north. So, if you are in the Spokane, Washington, region you have about 21° easterly declination, which means that you have to turn your map and compass 21° to the west or left to compensate for the declination. Once this is done the map is oriented to true north.

If you don't know where you are, finding yourself is only a matter of performing a few simple steps in a process called triangulation or resection. With your topographic map oriented on the ground in front of you, select a prominent terrain feature that you can see both on the ground and on the map. Shoot a bearing at it. We'll call this Point A.

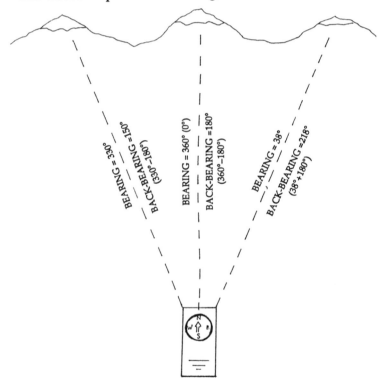

Triangulation (Resection) and Figuring Back-Bearings

Lay your compass on the map with the upper end of the straight edge on the top of Point A so that it makes an imaginary line from Point A back toward you. Trace a line along the straight edge to a point that you believe is well past your approximate position. Now select a second prominent terrain feature and do the same thing so that the two lines intersect. If truly prominent terrain features can't be found, then use a not so prominent feature. Just be sure it is recognizable on the map. Then repeat this procedure a third time. Also, whenever possible, select and use terrain features that are at least 45° apart, preferably more. The greater the angular separation, the lesser the error factor.

What you have now is three intersecting lines that form a small enclosure on the map. You are somewhere within that enclosure. (The chances of the three lines intersecting perfectly—not forming a small enclosure—are slim.) You have determined your position.

Could you determine your position by using only two features and two lines (back-bearings or back-azimuths)? Yes, but it is not as accurate as using three. This is known as biangulation or bisection. You could also use a single line and then terrain association to determine your exact position. This is done by examining the terrain around you in detail and then cross-checking with the map and the single back-bearing you have plotted. You know you are somewhere along that line, right? So now all you have to do is reference the terrain around you with the terrain you see around that back-bearing on the map. This is called single-line resection. Though all of these systems work, I recommend that whenever possible you use triangulation because it is more precise and reliable than the other two.

But what if you need to determine the location of a certain terrain feature on your topo map rather than find yourself? Is this even possible? Certainly. It's called intersection, and it is as simple to perform as a resection.

Let's say there is a cluster of hills, knolls, and broken terrain to your direct front, but you are having a tough time

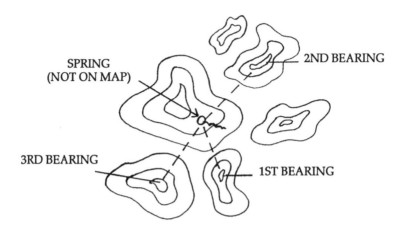

SPRING
(NOT ON MAP)

2ND BEARING

3RD BEARING

1ST BEARING

Intersection

determining which is which on your topographic map because of the jumbled lay of the land. Through your binoculars you see a spring located at the base of one of the numerous tiny knolls, and you are in dire need of water. You can see what the best route to the spring is, but you will be back this way and want to plot the spring on the map. You decide to run an intersection.

From where you are, take a bearing to the spring and plot the bearing on your map by tracing a straight line between you and it. Now move to another location at least 100 yards away from your original position from where you can still see the spring, and repeat the process. If possible do this a third time. Where the lines intersect (or create a small enclosure) is the location of the spring. Oh, did you remember to orient your map? If you didn't then your plot is wrong.

The importance of understanding these basic tenets cannot be overstated. Wayfinding is made much simpler when you truly understand how to orient (also called "lay" or "set") a topographic map and are comfortable doing so. If you aren't really sure how to perform a resection to locate yourself on a map, you are likely to begin doubting your decisions, the reliability of the map, and the accuracy of your compass. A lack of confidence breeds suspicion. Suspicion breeds self-doubt, which has an annoying habit of getting you lost.

To become proficient with the basic principles of map and compass work, *you must practice*. Time spent in the woods, even if those woods are right behind your house and you only have the chance to get out once in a while, will add up. Reading about how to do something is never enough. You have to gain experience. Reading a book on neurosurgery does not a surgeon make. So get out into the field at every opportunity.

CHAPTER FOUR

PUTTING IT ALL TOGETHER

S o far you have learned about your topographic map, its symbols, characteristics, benefits, and shortcomings. You have also learned about your compass, the different types available, and what makes each unique in some ways but always similar in others (they all have a north-seeking arrow, can be adversely affected by a local anomaly, etc.). And you now know how to orient your map by accounting for declination, how to find yourself and other features on the map, and why attention to detail and terrain association are so crucial to wayfinding.

You should also have noted that we have yet to do any wilderness wayfinding. You really haven't moved far at all, but for the bit on running an intersection. But fear not, because we are about to get underway, if I may use nautical parlance. We'll start slow and easy, then pick up the speed. If I become confused along the way, I'll just stash you in a thicket until I get my bearings, so don't think that I'm trying to get rid of you.

TRAVELING ON A BEARING

Before we can travel on a bearing we must first determine that bearing. A bearing is a straight line between two points that is referenced by a figure set to degrees magnetic or true. A bearing must have a figure of between 1° and 360° (sometimes referred to as 0°), inclusive. There is no such a thing as 361°, 422°, or any other bearing in excess of 360°.

To come up with a bearing between two points— a linear line of travel—first orient your map to true north and determine your position. Select the point you want to travel to. Trace a straight line between the two points and set your compass' straight edge along this line. Turn the bezel ring until the north-seeking arrow on the compass' needle lines up in the alignment lines. Now read the bearing at the head of the bezel ring, which is marked by the index line at the top center of the ring on the compass base. This is your true bearing. You don't have to add or subtract anything because your map is oriented to true north. (If you have the declination dialed in on your compensator compass' card, you don't have to rotate the map and compass together the number of degrees of declination for that area.)

Look out along that bearing and take note of what you see along that route. Is there a prominent or otherwise memorable landmark or feature along that path? If so, put your compass away and walk to that feature. There is no need to hold your compass out in front of you while traveling. When you get to that feature take the compass out again and shoot the bearing once more. Again, look for a prominent feature or landmark and go to it. Continue this for as long as it takes to get to the end of that leg, which refers to one bearing in a series of bearings you intend to take. Remember that the landmarks you use to guide you on the bearing might be as little as a few yards away or perhaps miles away. It all depends on the terrain, vegetation, and weather conditions. Be sure to select a feature that is easily distinguished from others around it. A fir tree that could be mistaken for another fir tree is not what you want.

I can't stress enough how essential it is for you to get an accurate bearing before stepping off. An error of 1° might seem inconsequential to you, but you must remember that the farther you travel on an erroneous bearing, the farther you will be off your planned destination at the end of that leg. A 1° error on a 100-yard leg won't throw you too far off and won't hurt you too much if you have no other legs to run. But if the leg is a mile long you are going to be quite a ways off course. And if you have other legs to run, you will be starting out on them off course unless you replot at the end of each leg, whereupon you should discover that you are off course.

You do not have to be standing at one end of a leg to determine the bearing from that point to another. With your map oriented, just pretend you are already at that point and get your bearing. This way you can plot legs for an entire route right from the start. However, as a precaution, always reorient yourself at the end of each leg. Also, recheck your bearing from time to time along each leg to ensure that local anomalies aren't throwing you off course.

JUDGING DISTANCE

To determine how far a certain leg is, all you must have is a pencil or pen and a piece of paper. Place the edge of the paper along your bearing between your starting and ending point. Place tick marks at each spot. Now set those marks along the bar scale you have chosen (yards, meters, or statute miles), and read what you have come up with. It is a common error to start at the far left side of a scale, the end that is broken down into fractions. Most scales, you will find, actually start a little ways inside at zero. You can also buy a map measure which is a wheel attached to a calibrated dial that gives you distance when run along the map. This is a particularly useful device when measuring distances along roads, trails, and other routes of travel that are not straight.

But one thing that the paper and map measure methods don't tell you is *true distance*, that is, distance that takes into account the lay of the land. Both the paper and map measure method give you a distance that assumes the ground is flat, when, in reality, if the ground isn't flat you are traveling farther.

Though it isn't nearly as accurate as the map measure wheel, the paper method can also be used to determine distance along routes of travel that are curved. Place the first tick mark at the starting point and the next one at the first curve (no matter how slight). Place additional ticks as the curve continues, being sure to go along the outside edge of the curve. At the end of the curve just continue along and place the next tick mark at the beginning of the next curve, and so on until you come to the end of your route.

Still with me so far? Good. Let's move on.

WAY-POINTS

After you plot your bearing and before you set off, study your intended route of travel very well. What does your topographic map tell you about the route? Look at the contour lines and get an idea about the lay of the land along the way. Are there streams? Ridges? Draws? Fingers? Saddles? Depressions? Cliffs? *Study the map.* Look for terrain features that you believe will be readily recognized when you come upon them and note each one's relationship to other features in the area. These become your way-points. Way-points are great for keeping you on course and add no small measure of self-confidence to the wilderness wayfinder. As you pass one way-point you will find that you automatically start thinking about the next one. You begin to anticipate its appearance and form a mental image in your mind of how the feature will look when you get to it. I have found that this mental image is almost always wrong. This fact can cause you to begin to doubt yourself if you aren't careful. The map says your next way-point is a stream in a draw. When you get there you find that the draw is barely that and the stream is no more than a barely discernible trickle—not at all what you expected to find.

This is precisely what happened to a marine reconnaissance team I was grading in a remote corner of the Hawaiian island of Molokai in 1980. The team leader had plotted a way-point that the map said was a stream in a draw. He told his point man this after leaving the previous way-point, and the marine began looking for it once the pacer's (the marine two men behind the point man; the marine immediately behind him is the navigator) count told him they were getting close. The point man had a certain mental image in mind and walked right over the stream, which was almost dry but for a tiny trickle below the rocks. I stopped him and asked where he was going. When I told him that he had just stepped over the stream he was looking for, he didn't believe me. So I had him do a resection to determine his position and told the navigator and pacer to find out where we were by dead reckoning. Both came up with the same answer: we were at the way-point.

Attention to detail is vital to a thorough map study. That attention to detail must also be used when looking for certain terrain features on the ground. If you are weak at one or both, problems will arise.

Ten years after I left Hawaii I was asked to set up a land navigation course for newly certified survival instructors at the Navy Survival School in Maine. The individual routes I planned were aggressive and designed to test the instructors' ability to wayfind over unfamiliar terrain that was rugged and demanding. The course took five days to complete, and on the morning of the fifth day all but one of the two-man/woman teams had radioed in that they were either approaching their final check-point or had already reached it and were heading for the base camp. I radioed the team that hadn't called in yet and asked where they were.

"Well, we aren't really sure," came the meek response.

Oh, good, I thought to myself. "Alright, where were you last?"

"Up on Poplar Ridge at the lean-to."

I plotted this on my map. "What bearing were you on when you left there, when did you leave there, and what did you see along the way?" They told me, and I plotted the bearing on my map. "Okay, what do you see now?"

"Lots of trees."

Oh, good. "Have you crossed a major stream since you left the lean-to?"

"No."

Ah. "Do you think you were true to your bearing?"

"Yeah, we think so."

At this point I told them to continue heading east until they hit the major stream I was talking about, Orbeton Stream, at which time they should continue a short distance past it and hit the trail along the rim of the shallow valley. Then they should turn left and continue along the trail until they hit Redington Pond, at the far end of which was the base camp.

Two hours or so went by and I hadn't heard from them, so I dialed them up.

"Where are you?"

"Heading up the stream. We couldn't find the trail after we crossed over it so we went back to the stream and are following it up to the pond."

"How long have you been following the stream?"

"Almost two hours."

Oh, good. At this point I knew we still had a problem because they should have reached the pond long ago.

"Stop," I told them. "You aren't on Orbeton Stream. You are on one of its feeder creeks. Don't move. We'll come and get you.

"But you don't know where we are!"

"We'll find you. Stay put."

Larry Small and I headed down the trail past the pond and along Orbeton Stream. We went about 400 meters down the trail and Larry cut into the woods toward the stream to try and cut some sign. He passed over the stream heading generally west until he began

Wherever you see the great blue heron, water is nearby.

crossing some feeder creeks, the second one of which
had a clear, fresh bootprint. One minute later he was

49

laughing in the faces of the two sheepish instructors. They never lived it down.

The mistakes they made were easy ones. They weren't keeping a pace count or using any type of way-point system to keep track of where they were. They weren't 100-percent sure that they had remained true to their bearing. They mistook a feeder creek for the stream I had sent them in search of and failed to note that the feeder creek wasn't flowing in the right direction. Had they done a good map study they wouldn't have become disoriented in the first place. The other mistakes merely added to the problem.

SUPPLEMENTAL SIGHT AND SOUND CUES

In between way-points you should be looking and listening for what I call supplemental sight and sound cues. These are not plotted way-points but rather selected terrain features that let you know you are still generally on course. They supplement your way-points, but never replace them altogether. A supplemental sight cue might be the ridge you need to keep to your right to stay within the corridor you have chosen. Or it might be the snow-capped volcano you know you must keep to your back if you want to stay on a westerly course. A sound cue is a terrain feature that tells you where it is at by making some sort of noise. This is usually a fast-moving stream or river, but it could also be a distant highway or the crash of the surf on a far-off beach.

Contour itself can be used as a supplemental sight cue. When doing the map, study be sure to take special note of the subtle and not so subtle undulations in the land. If you expect to be on a long, gentle downhill slope after 100-meters of travel, but instead you find that a major chasm has opened before you, recheck the map and recheck your compass. You may have been standing on a lodestone which threw your compass off. You may have inadvertently shot the bearing with a tilted compass. Or perhaps that camera hanging around your neck drew the north-seeking arrow to it.

LOOKING BACK

Clever woodsmen know how important it is to be aware of what is behind you at all times. This might be a deer that stepped out onto the trail as you passed by, an irritated grizzly that is thinking of you as an hors d'oeuvre, or a prominent terrain feature that you could use as a supplemental sight cue. During your map study, be sure to note what features you should be able to see behind you from various vantage points.

Speaking of back, you can arrive at a back-bearing by a simple mathematical formula (it has to be simple for me to understand). If your bearing is less than 180°, add 180°; if it is more than 180°, subtract 180°. If it is 180°, your back-bearing is obviously 360° or 0°.

ODDS AND ENDS

Before we wade any deeper into the morass, a few odds and ends. Carry afield with you a few 5" x 8" laminated index cards and a grease pencil or alcohol pen to make terrain sketches with. These also come in handy during rescue work.

Your compass should remain fixed somehow to your body. Tie it to a belt loop, keep it around your neck, tie it to your pack, or whatever else you feel comfortable with, just as long as it is secured somehow. Compasses have a funny way of staying where you last put them. They are particularly fond of sitting on rocks, logs, car hoods, and just about any other platform of sorts. They will never follow you when you leave them somewhere, either. Even the most expensive, bodacious compass on the market is totally untrainable. I know, I've tried. So attach your compass to yourself lest it be found by some archaeologist a few thousand years from now who will no doubt think it

Broken terrain can both help and hinder your wayfinding.

to be some sort of religious talisman designed to ward off evil wood spirits.

Never trust the weather. Before you make camp for the evening, get your bearing for the morning and write it down on one of those index cards. This way, if the weather goes bad on you but you still want to move on, you already have your starting bearing. And it's written down on a piece of paper that won't run in the rain.

CHAPTER FIVE

TRICKS OF THE TRADE

N o doubt you realize by now that we still haven't done anything wild and crazy. We've been sticking to the basics. You now know how to shoot bearings and travel along them, use way-points and supplemental sight and sound cues, and so on. You're feeling pretty confident and want to play rough. So be it.

Robert W. Service's eerie tale of life in the wilderness, "The Lone Trail," says it all:

> And sometimes it leads to the desert, and the
> tongue swells out of the mouth,
> And you stagger blind to the mirage, to die in
> the mocking drouth.
> And sometimes it leads to the mountain, to the
> light of the lone camp-fire,
> And you gnaw your belt in the anguish of
> hunger-goaded desire.
> And sometimes it leads to the Southland, to the
> swamp where the orchid glows,
> And you rave to your grave with the fever, and
> they rob the corpse for its clothes.
> And sometimes it leads to the Northland, and

the scurvy softens your bones,
And your flesh dints in like putty, and you spit
    out your teeth like stones.
And sometimes it leads to a coral reef in the
    wash of a weedy sea,
And you sit and stare at the empty glare where
    the gulls wait greedily.
And sometimes it leads to an Arctic trail
    and the snows where your torn feet freeze,
And you whittle away the useless clay, and
    crawl on your hands and knees . . .

Sounds like a pretty good time, eh? Well, here we go.

CONTOURING

Put your compass away. No, don't set it on that rock. Put it in your pocket and tie the cord to your belt loop. That's better. Now it will be there when you next need it.

Contouring is another one of those skills that requires attention to detail and a thorough map study. It does not require a compass in its pure form. It does demand a well-developed sense of terrain association, though.

Contouring is traveling over undeveloped or unspoiled terrain by using a knowledge of the lay of the land to guide you. You do not shoot bearings. You do not run on arrow-straight legs plotted neatly on your trusty topographic map. You do not shoot a resection or triangulate to find yourself on the map. You use the terrain as your guide.

Spooky, huh?

Let's go back to the beginning. Take out your map and orient it. Find your destination. Now closely examine—study—every terrain feature and nuance that may be able to guide you along your way. Determine what the best route appears to be, and always have a second in mind should your first choice not pan out. Are there any streams along the way? How many? How far apart are they spaced? What hills or peaks do you expect to be able to see, either the entire time or at certain vantage points? Are there series of spurs or some other repetitive terrain features that are easily recognized off to one side, ahead, or behind you? Is there a lake, pond, or river in the area that you can see from high points? A good map study will answer all these questions and help you in planning your route.

Once you step, off keep your map handy and folded so that the specific area you are in is exposed. Refer to your topo map frequently and keep track of what features you use as way-points and supplemental sight and sound cues. If the region you are in has many small streams, keep an accurate count of them as you pass. Check the surrounding terrain as you do this. Make sure it matches what the map says. This system of checks and balances can save you a lot of time and trouble.

Think of contouring as a pinball game with you being the pinball. The flippers, walls, rubber bands, and other features of the game keep the pinball within the field of play. Terrain features keep the wayfinder who is contouring within the field of play, so to speak.

DEAD RECKONING

How can you determine your position—find yourself—along a route of travel when landmarks to shoot a resection off of are not available or can't be seen due to weather or vegetation restrictions? Can this be done? Yes. It is called dead reckoning, and it can "fix your pos" ("pos," pronounced "pawz," is wayfinding lingo for finding your position) quickly and accurately if you know how.

To dead reckon you must: (A) know exactly from where you started, (B) know and be sure of your pace count, and (C) remain true to your bearing, i.e., don't stray off course. Additionally, you should use terrain association to corroborate your dead reckoning findings.

To dead reckon you must keep an accurate pace count along your route of travel, being sure to stick to your bearing from a known point. At any point on the leg you can use your pace count to determine how far along the leg you have traveled. Now it is only a matter of using the appropriate bar scale to plot how far you have gone. Could it be this simple? Yes, but only over flat, unbroken ground in good weather and minimal vegetation. What does all this have to do with it?

Your pace count can and will be affected by all these factors and more. Any terrain feature other than a pan-flat plain will cause your pace count to vary. Uphill travel will almost always shorten your stride, while downhill travel can either shorten it or lengthen it depending on the surface. Inclement or extreme weather conditions will also alter your pace. Rain and blowing snow will cause you to lower your head and shorten your step. Restrictive clothing will shorten your stride, as will dense vegetation. Your physical condition plays a role, too. If you overexert yourself your stride will be chopped. A cold or other malady will do the same.

Experience goes a long ways here. Seasoned wayfinders know how to account for all these factors when pace counting. It takes time, but you will get the hang of it. Terrain association, as mentioned above, is a kind of insurance when dead reckoning. If your pace count says that you should be about a "click" (1,000 meters) south of a volcano, but a nudist colony is there instead, then you have gone wrong somewhere. (Then again, maybe you haven't.) It should be obvious at this point that way-points, supplemental sight and sound cues, and an in-depth map study will all assist you when dead reckoning.

THE PACE COUNT

Remember that movie where the good guys find a treasure map (with the location of the treasure marked by a bold-faced "X"), and part of the means of discovering its hiding place was walking north from the horse head-shaped rock exactly 20 paces? Remember when they counted off 20 steps and started digging, but found nothing? Where did they go wrong? Easy. They took 20 steps instead of 20 paces. A *pace* is two steps, not one. Every time a particular foot hits the ground in a normal gait is one pace. Now, the next time you find a treasure map you won't make the same mistake those greenhorns did.

Two people are unlikely to have the same pace. This means that you are going to have to determine for yourself how many paces it takes you to walk 100 yards. Get thee down to yon football field and walk from one end to the other, excluding the end zones. Walk at a normal pace and keep track of how many times your right or left foot strikes the ground. When you get to the other end remember that number and turn around and do it again. You may find that your count differs by a step or two. Split the difference. This is your pace count.

While traveling, you must have a system of some sort to keep track of how many paces/100-yard increments you have traveled. One time-honored means is to tie a cord to your belt loop and tie one overhand knot in it every time you go 100 yards. You might want to put a tick on a piece of paper for every 100 yards, or use a ticket-taker's thumb clicker to keep track. Whatever works for you.

Pacing can be monotonous. That's why it is a good idea to switch pacers when in a group. If you are on your own, well, that's the way it goes sometimes. After a while you will find that you are keeping an accurate count while not even thinking about it. It becomes natural. You will learn how to adjust your count for the factors affecting it. This, too, will become natural.

OFFSET NAVIGATION

Wayfinding sometimes requires you to find a comparatively small object or feature. This might be a cache you have hidden in some inconspicuous spot, a concealed spring behind a remote cabin in Maine's Redington Pond Range, or some other thing of value. Pin-point navigation is not always the best solution and in fact is sometimes simply not possible or feasible. This is when offset navigation comes into play.

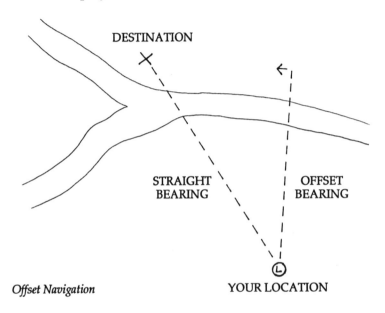

Offset Navigation

Offset navigation is a method of wayfinding where you intentionally plot your course to one side or another of a feature so that when you reach that feature you will know which way to turn for the final short leg of your route to reach your destination.

Let's say that you have deposited a cache with some things you are in dire need of in a certain location on the west side of a stream, about 100 yards north of the only 270° bend in that stream in this region. Attempting to strike that cache dead-on from a great distance isn't smart in this case because the terrain could, and probably would, cause you to overshoot or otherwise miss your mark. The solution is offset navigation.

You orient your map, do a map study, and plot a course that will have you strike the stream just south of the 270° bend. Once you get to the stream you cross over to the west side. Now you know that all you need to do is turn to the north and follow the stream up to the cache.

What you have done is figured in an intentional error of sorts to assist you in your wayfinding.

Use some common sense when you figure in this "error." Remember that the greater the distance, the

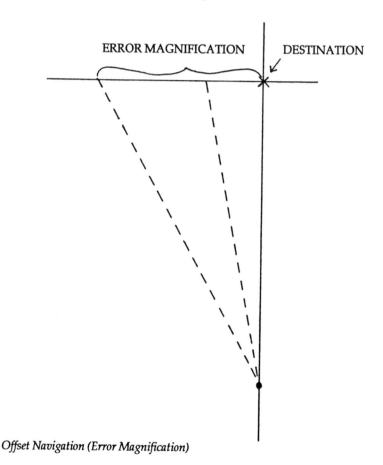

Offset Navigation (Error Magnification)

smaller the error or offset should be, because the farther you travel on the offset leg the farther you will be off your final destination. To show this better, get a pencil and paper. Draw a straight line from top to bottom one inch in from the right margin. Now draw a straight line from left to right one inch down from the top margin. Now place a dot on the vertical line one inch up from the bottom. This is you. Where the vertical and horizontal lines intersect at the top right of the paper is the destination that you want to reach by offset navigation. Draw another line, this one from the dot to a point one inch to the left of this intersection. Now draw one from the dot to a point three inches to the left of the intersection. As you can see, the greater the distance traveled while offsetting, the greater the distance will be that you are from your true destination.

DETOURING

Yet another trick of the wilderness wayfinding trade is called detouring.

Detouring is using two or more legs to take you in directions other than directly toward your final destination for the day. They are plotted and designed to move you around an obstacle safely and effectively and then get you back on your original bearing.

If you already have a little experience in navigation you may be saying that you need three such legs to run a detour. Wrong. You can get away with only two in many situations and may need several in others. It all depends on the situation, your map study, and you.

TWO-LEG DETOUR

Your map study has shown a problem. A tremendous swamp lies directly in the path you want to take, which—but for the swamp—appears to be an excellent route. You

Two-Leg Detour

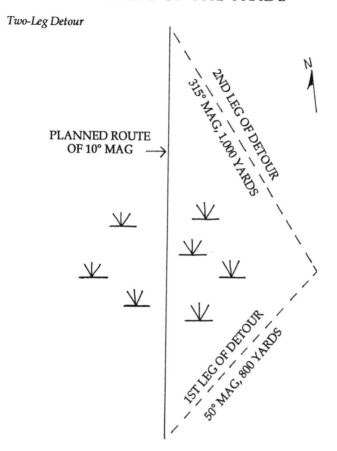

PLANNED ROUTE
OF 10° MAG →

2ND LEG OF DETOUR
315° MAG, 1,000 YARDS

N

1ST LEG OF DETOUR
50° MAG, 800 YARDS

don't want to traverse the swamp, so you elect to go around it. You intend to take a detour.

At a selected point along your route of travel approaching the swamp, you stop and orient yourself to make sure this is the right jumping-off spot. You have plotted a two-leg detour, the first of which is 800 yards on a 50° bearing (40° east of your bearing of 10°). The end of this first detour leg will put you on a knoll with a draw and two fingers (spurs) running off the eastern slope. You move out, keeping a pace count and using good way-points and terrain association plus supplementary sight and sound cues to guide you. When you reach the knoll you orient yourself again and verify your position. Then you set off on the second leg of your detour, a 1,000-yard leg that runs on a 315° heading. You take off, keeping a pace count, etc. When you reach the 1,000-yard point you stop and verify your position. You should be back along your original route of travel, only farther to the north and on the far side of the swamp. You have detoured around it. Now get back on your original bearing and move out.

THREE-LEG OR TRI-90° DETOUR

The same rules apply as with the two-leg detour, but here you are running three-detour legs, each of which is 90° off the last.

To make it simple to understand, imagine you are on a bearing of 360°. You come to the swamp, gorge, Iraqi

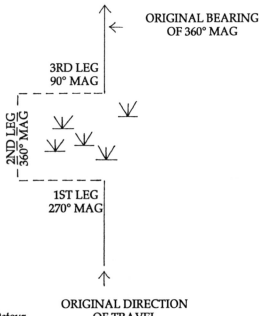

ORIGINAL BEARING
OF 360° MAG

3RD LEG
90° MAG

2ND LEG
360° MAG

1ST LEG
270° MAG

ORIGINAL DIRECTION
OF TRAVEL

Three-Leg or Tri-90° Detour

Intelligence Center (now there's a contradiction in terms for you), or some other obstacle you want to avoid. You have selected the three-leg or tri-90° detour method. You see by your map study that the best way to go is to the west. This makes your first detour leg 270°. You move along this course until you determine that you are past the westerly extent of the obstacle. Verify your position and set your next leg, which isssss . . . 360°, right! (If Don Rickles were here he would say, "You get a cookie," but he isn't here and I don't have any cookies, so just keep reading.) You are now moving parallel to your original bearing. Once again you move until you feel you are above the northern extent of the obstacle, whereupon you verify your position and take up your third detour bearing of 90°. Now you're heading back toward your original route of travel. When your pace count or whatever tells you that you have reached that original route of travel, get back on it. You have detoured around the obstacle by forming an open-ended box of sorts.

CONTOURING

Your map study and personal experience may indicate that you should simply contour around the obstacle. Frankly, this is often the easiest way to get around something. You don't have to do fancy compass work, keep a boring pace count, or perform intricate mathematical formulas. You just go around.

GAME TRAILS

Game trails can prove to be a tremendous boon to the wilderness wayfinder. They can also be of no use whatsoever. For some reason, animals don't create trails with humans in mind. They're funny that way. Maybe this is one of their clever little ways of getting back at us for eating them.

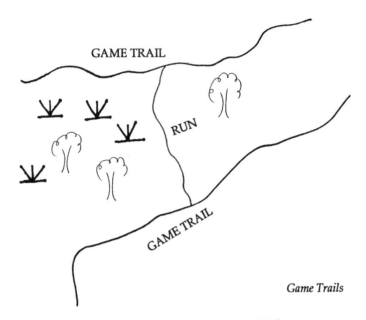

Game Trails

RISE- AND DROP-TRAILING

In regions with animal species such as moose, elk, mule deer, and other good-sized creatures that habitually use major trail systems to get from one place to another, you can use their trails as wilderness highways. If you are heading up a heavily wooded slope, look for a trail heading into the highlands. Get on this trail and stay on it until it turns downhill or fades away. At this point turn back uphill, cutting through the woods until you strike another trail that is heading uphill. Continue this technique until you reach the elevation you desire. The same technique can be used to get down into the lowlands, of course, merely in reverse.

Wild game is finely tuned to the environment. They create trails for reasons. I have heard it said and seen it written that a game trail always leads to water. Nothing could be farther from the truth.

Two game trails that converge will often lead to water,

Moose make excellent trails that the wayfinder can use too.

this is true. I might be willing to say that they usually do.
However, a game trail might lead to a shelter area, feeding

ground, breeding ground, or any combination of these. Furthermore, that trail you are on may not be a trail at all but rather a run, which is a path used by a single primary species (and a few others) that connects two major trails. The difference in appearance between a major trail and a run is very noticeable. A major trail is commonly used by several species: a coyote pack, white-tailed deer, red fox, and snowshoe hare may all use a trail created by moose, for instance. But a run between two moose trails will often be used by only the moose or perhaps a select few others. Runs are frequently temporary, too, whereas major trails are more permanent.

TERRAIN AND VEGETATION

Woodswise wayfinders know that terrain can and often does have an effect on what type of vegetation grows where and how dense it gets. Choosing the wrong terrain to traverse can lead to exhaustion, frustration, and even danger. If you are not familiar with the different types of vegetation and species of plants that live in your region and how the terrain can radically affect its growth, then learn. Do this before you find yourself relying on your wilderness wayfinding skills in a life or death situation.

One example of this is the well-known fact that vegetation tends to grow more heavily on the north side of a hill or mountain than on the south. By the same token, the windward side of a hill (most often the western side) will likely have denser flora than the leeward (eastern) side.

The tops of fingers are often easier to travel than the bottoms of draws. Water flowing down the draw, no matter how slight a flow, can create an almost impenetrable wall of vegetation. I once made the mistake of bushwhacking down a draw running into the Redington Valley in Maine that began in the saddle between Saddleback Junior and The Horn. You would think I would have known better, especially since I had just scratched and clawed my way up the north face of Saddleback Junior that morning. There I had discovered for myself that krumholz (extremely dense stands of twisted and deformed fir and spruce found just below timberline at higher elevations) are not fun to crawl through and that terrain most certainly does affect vegetation. But nooooo. I was a marine—and a "recon" marine at that—which meant I could go wherever I wanted at any time I so desired. No one told me that this rule didn't apply 100 percent of the time. By the time I reached the valley floor I looked as if a hormone-imbalanced hen Sasquatch had had her way with me, repeatedly. It was not pretty.

Traversing a slope is taxing. If you can, get either to the top or to the bottom. You also stand a much better chance of spraining an ankle while traversing a slope. And another thing: if you are on a bearing and traversing a slope at the same time, you tend to fall off your bearing, i.e., gravitate down the slope a little at a time without noticing it. If the slope is a long one and you don't discover this mistake, well . . .

I have spent quite a lot of time in the jungles of the Philippines. Of the many lessons I learned there, one that stands out is that sometimes you find routes that make travel and wayfinding easier in places you don't expect them to be. Streambeds afforded me some excellent routes, particularly in the drier months when the rains slacked off and the streams subsided. Many of these streambeds were inundated with large, smooth rocks that could fairly easily be negotiated by hopping from one to another. This was a lot easier than busting brush in the jungle lining the stream banks. Our porters gave us the idea after we set off through the bush. We hadn't gone 10 meters before the honcho recommended that we get in the streambed rather than play Bwana in the bushes.

DOWN THE DRAIN

The drainage pattern of the terrain can prove beneficial to

travel and wayfinding. In unfamiliar terrain, a detailed map study will reveal the region's drainage pattern, be it trellis, branching, parallel, radial, or a combination of two or more of these. Some drainage patterns lend themselves nicely to navigation and wayfinding. Others don't. But all can be used effectively if you do a good map study or are otherwise familiar with the region. Don't depend on the drainage pattern to assist you unless you know what you are doing. In a radial drainage pattern it is easy—very easy—to confuse one stream for another. This means that you could inadvertently be going "one-eighty out" (180° off the direction you want to go in), and end up in another world.

Before we move on, let me stress that there is no such thing as cheating at wayfinding, unless you are in an orienteering event.

In wayfinding, how you play the game is irrelevant. The important thing is to win. Cheat all you like. Heck, you might even want to think about buying an altimeter. They aren't very expensive and are extremely useful in wayfinding. Dead reckoning, resection, detouring, and offset navigation are just a small sample of wayfinding skills that are made more accurate with the help of a pocket altimeter.

CHAPTER SIX

THE ENVIRONMENT ANGLE

Different environments often mean different approaches to wayfinding. How you wayfind in the Malaysian jungle will unlikely be the same as in the Gobi Desert. The same holds true for the Everglades and Great Plains, Kenyan savanna and Alaskan tundra, and Australia's King Leopold Ranges and California chaparral. Like the creatures that dwell there, you must adapt to each environment. Failure to do so means death for these creatures. It could mean the same for you.

There is no one trick of the trade that will make every wilderness trip you make smooth and easy. However, certain principles can be applied to all situations involving wayfinding and navigation:

(1) The chances of your dying in the wilderness because you have become lost is very remote. Many more people die from being struck by lightning in this country every year than from becoming lost and suffering the consequences.

(2) Planning will prevent almost all emergency situations in the wilderness. Some, however, such as your appendix exploding or being struck by a stray fragment from Halley's comet, are unavoidable.

Marine 1st Sgt. Rick Buchikos (in camouflage) with Spanish Legionnaires and a tasty bunny in the Spanish countryside.

(3) Humans are remarkably resourceful. The body can withstand much more punishment and abuse than you might think. Some types of abuse are likelier to cause severe damage more quickly than others. One of these is dehydration.

(4) Don't panic. True, this is sometimes easier said than done. But when you think about it, how many people have you heard of who died in the wilderness recently?

(5) Common sense and preparation are two of the three most important assets a person can have in the wilderness. The third is a powerful will to live.

WAYFINDING TIPS FOR DIFFERENT ENVIRONMENTS

Desert

I can vividly recall seeing the Arabian Desert for the first time. It was from an altitude of about 37,000 feet in a chartered jet heading for al Jubayl. It was December 31, 1990.

I slid the plastic window shade up and gawked out the window. The desert pulled away in all directions, flat, tan, and utterly empty. Devoid of life. Nothingness. Or so it appeared from this height. Many thoughts flooded my beleaguered brain at this moment, one of which was: how in the name of Beau Geste was I going to find my way around down there? I was raised in the backwoods of Maine, not the shifting sands of Arabia! Ohhh, I was in big trouble.

But the desert wasn't completely flat, utterly empty, or without life. People lived down there, had for thousands of years. They figured out how to find their way from one side of the desert to the other. I would too.

Once we had made our way out into the desert proper, after a two week stay in the Marine Expeditionary Camp outside of the Saudi port city of al Jubayl, I began wandering away from my unit whenever I could, alone. Sometimes I would venture only a few hundred meters; other times I would go for quite a ways before I turned around and headed back. The company commander didn't like the idea of my strolling around by myself, but I think he knew the importance of someone knowing the outlying terrain and how to navigate without the use of fancy equipment linked somehow to some satellites orbiting the planet that told you where you were.

The first thing I realized on my initial walkabout was that the desert is anything but a lifeless void, and it is covered with subtle hints of movement: an ancient camel trail here, a small rock outcropping there (used for centuries as a navigational way-point). How could I know such a thing? I sat by the rocks for a spell one day waiting for the distant dust cloud I could see on the horizon to reach me. It was a small band of nomadic Bedouins and their omnipresent dromedary camels (one-humpers are dromedary camels found in North Africa and Southwest Asia; two-humpers are bactrian camels native to northern Asia). Naturally they stopped to see what idiot was sitting on the rock outcropping in the middle of East Overshoe, Arabia.

Their English was terrible (imagine that!), and my Arabic was a little rusty, so we all decided that the time-honored practice of sign language would be used. Not the kind deaf people use. The kind used by people who have no idea what the other is saying because they can't understand a single word of the other's ridiculous language. First, they wanted to see my rifle and examine the rest of my gear, which I was happy to allow. (I made sure the weapon, an M16A2, wasn't loaded and was on "safe.") After they all took turns aiming at each other and pretending to blow each other away, we got down to some serious sign language. I wanted to know how they navigated across the desert and showed them my map and compass to get them thinking along these lines. It took a good 10 minutes, but I finally understood that they used the stars at night (which I already knew) and the sun, landmarks, and an intricate series of trails during the day.

The desert is much more than a lifeless void.

My map had Arabic place-names on it, and when they saw these it was fairly easy to get me to understand about their wayfinding. When they figured out that I wanted to know how long they had been using the rock outcropping as a way-point, they replied in very broken English "forever" and "always."

I also asked them why they dressed in black, which I always thought attracted heat. It does, but the almost constant breeze doesn't allow the heat to stick to their clothing. It literally blows it off.

Desert travel requires attention to detail in the extreme. Deserts are subtle places that demand determination, savvy, and common sense. Learn the desert's ways before you go there. You'll thank me later.

MOUNTAINS

A substantial percentage of my wayfinding experience has been gleaned in one mountainous region or another. I have been very fortunate to have trod through mountain ranges from Korea to Japan, Germany to Scandinavia, Maine to California, and many other locales. And I've become unsure as to my precise whereabouts in them all. This makes me a warehouse of advice on how not to do things. However, over the years I have managed to figure out how to tell people to avoid the mistakes I have made in such a way that they remember most of what I say. That explains this latest book.

Mountain travel is steeped in lore. This is no surprise. Tales of mountain ranges and the men and women who traveled them in the last century make for some fabulous reading. Perhaps one day folks will read about an adventure you had in the mountains.

What advice can I give you about wayfinding in the mountains? As an overview, pay attention to your map. *Study it.* Trust your compass. Believe in yourself as well as your map and compass. Don't spend too much time worrying about being eaten by a bear or mountain lion. Use nature's paths.

Some finer points include:

(1) knowing that moss usually grows thickest on the north side of trees,

(2) avoiding walking straight up a slope; angle off and zig-zag up it, resting when you feel the need,

(3) recognizing that avalanches can often be avoided but not always. A moderate slope with minimal vegetation on the lee side of a mountain during or immediately after a storm, especially if it just warmed up substantially after a cold snap, is bad ju-ju,

(4) using the terrain to your advantage; if you begin to feel that it is defeating you, it may already have,

(5) remembering that mountain ranges have a tendency to form their own weather patterns. You've been warned.

Injuries are common among mountain travelers who are new or unaccustomed to such travel. A dose of caution and common sense goes a long way toward preventing problems. Don't take unnecessary risks. That's how people get killed.

Acute Mountain Sickness (AMS), High Altitude Pulmonary Edema (HAPE), and High Altitude Cerebral Edema (HACE) are three illnesses that you must be ready for. Don't fool with any of them.

Though technical mountain climbing skills aren't required for wilderness wayfinding, they do build confidence and serve in emergencies. A basic course in rock climbing and rappelling is advisable.

JUNGLE AND RAINFOREST

The jungle and the rainforest are two different environments, but I've lumped them both together in this text because most people associate the two. In reality, their differences are legion.

When most people hear the word "jungle," they picture a tropical forest with dense understory; screaming, colorful fowl; a prodigious array of snakes and other reptiles; and dangerous mammals such as the jaguar. This is often a pretty good description, too.

The terrain a jungle is situated on may be flat, or it may be hilly, even mountainous. In any case, though, one of the primary features of all jungles is thick vegetation. Whether the jungle you find yourself in is as flat as a table or as rugged as the Badlands, the flora growing thereon is going to affect your wayfinding. If you can't see more than a few feet in front of you, you had better be sharp when it comes to detailed terrain association and other fine aspects of wilderness navigation.

Dense jungle vegetation requires the would-be Tarzan to stick tightly to bearings when on them. This type of flora is uncannily able to adjust your course for you without your knowing or approving of it. A dozen unaccounted-for *minor* bearing shifts equate to a *major* problem at the end of that leg. In the jungle, navigational mistakes have a way of multiplying resultant problems exponentially. This can turn out to be a life-threatening situation. But the jungle is navigable. Bogey and Kate did it by using the rivers. So did Stanley, Kenneth Clark, and who knows how many other explorers who brashly strode into an emerald green abyss in search of destiny, Livingston, the Seven Cities of Cíbola, and innumerable other treasures.

Rivers are one means of wayfinding in the jungle, but you must have an exceptionally good idea of the region's drainage patterns to put them to good use. This means that you are either going to have to have a good, current topographic map, a native guide who knows the region like the proverbial back of his hand, or some other dependable knowledge of the lay of the land and waters. The jungle is unforgiving. You can't afford many mistakes. Seriously.

The rain forest is different. Impenetrable understory isn't the norm, but rather fairly open vegetation down below with triple or quadruple canopy above. This multiple-umbrella effect—with tall trees sporting widespread, leafy branches that block out the sun and allow only dappled sunlight to invade the shadows of the ground below —means that shooting a resection is almost always out of the question. The stars can rarely be used since you can't see more than a tiny section of the night sky at any one time, and the weather—the weather!—is, well, a little damp.

In the rain forest you must take advantage of every opportunity to orient yourself. (The same is true of the jungle.) Water systems can be used effectively, too. However, caution is paramount when using the rivers. Many species of potentially deadly animals live on, in, or near the rivers and streams. The Orinoco River croc, one of the world's largest, lives in the river basin of the same name in South America. The Gabon viper of West African forests will strike instantly with no provocation; his fangs are two inches long and are attached to poison glands filled with a heinous juice that has both hemotoxic and neurotoxic properties. You get the picture.

I am not going to go into further detail giving specific advice for each type of region. I can't see breaking it down into natural vegetation zones coupled with various predominant terrain features, such as subtropical Caribbean thorn forests or ice and alpine tundra regions. The principles of wayfinding remain constant no matter where you are, to tell you the truth. It is up to you to adapt to them and make the principles herein work for wherever you are at the time.

CHAPTER SEVEN

PRIMITIVE MEANS

I magine navigating for years and years in utter wilderness with which you are completely unfamiliar. You make your way by your wits and wiles, not only wayfinding but surviving from day to day. You are your own grocer, butcher, farmer, doctor, engineer, and counselor. You are the one responsible for your life and to a much greater degree than we know today.

This was the life of the American pilgrims, explorers, and pioneers of the last three centuries. So it was with like folk on every continent. Even today, we still find people tucked away in remote corners of the world who still practice wayfinding and survival in general on a daily basis. We see them on National Geographic specials and think, "My God, how can they live like that?" Yet this is precisely how we lived not so long ago.

Progress and civilization (as we know it) tend to mask the skills our ancestors used every day. Our creature comforts become seeming necessities rather than the mere amenities they really are. Nevertheless, primitive wayfinding skills are still with us today as a result of a small handful of writers and educators who believe that preserving this knowledge base is essential to our future. The past lights the way to tomorrow.

THE SHADOW KNOWS

We'll talk about the stars in detail in a little while, but there is one star that stands out from most of the others: Sol.

Sol (our sun), the nearest star to Earth, has been guiding wayfarers for eons. The number of ancient peoples who used the sun to navigate across vast expanses of ocean and through the wildest terrain imaginable will likely never be known in full. Archaeologists and anthropologists are still discovering civilizations that were temporarily lost to eternity who used the sun to get around. Sometimes way around. Some ancient peoples who worshipped the sun, such as the Aztecs of current-day Mexico, knew the sun as Teotl, though they also had many lesser gods. And the ancient Sumerians believed the sun was the Big Kahuna, too, so to speak. Though we are now pretty sure that the sun isn't a god, we do know that it is a relative constant, as are all the stars in our galaxy. This isn't to say that stars don't come and go. They do. But red giants, white dwarfs, and black dwarfs don't happen in our galactic neighborhood on a daily basis, so we are fairly well assured that ol' Teotl isn't going to reach critical mass suddenly in the very near future.

Because the sun and the Earth's rotation around it are constants, we know that every day the sun is going to rise in the east and set in the west. This means that shadows fall from west to east. From this deduction we can determine due north.

THE SHADOW STICK

Should you have ignored my advice and somehow attached your compass to your body so that it is now decorating a pack rat's den in the Mojave Desert, you are going to have to find some other means of determining north and the other cardinal directions. One such means is the shadow stick.

PRIMITIVE MEANS

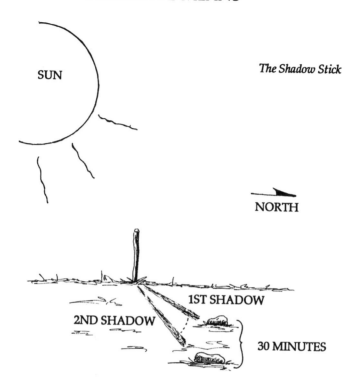

The Shadow Stick

SUN

NORTH

1ST SHADOW

2ND SHADOW

30 MINUTES

Find a straight stick about a meter long and jam it into the ground in a spot where sunlight is falling. At the end of the shadow it casts place a pine cone, prickly pear fruit, rock, or some other object that is going to stay put for a while. Now wait for half an hour or so for the shadow to move. (Keep in mind that the shadow is moving from west to east.) After it has shifted enough, place a second object at the tip of that shadow. There is no need to draw a line between the two shadows. Step in between the stick and the objects with your back to the stick. Put the tip of your left foot at the first object, the tip of your right at the second. Look forward. You are facing due north.

From this point it is a simple matter to determine the remaining three cardinal directions of east (to your right), south (behind you), and west (to your left).

The shadow stick method of cardinal direction determination is useful in determining only cardinal, and perhaps the intercardinal directions: (northeast, southeast, southwest, and northwest). You can't determine precise compass bearings with it. However, it can be used very effectively with terrain association, a map study, and other wayfinding tools. It obviously has one drawback: you can't use it unless a shadow can be produced. Overcast days that deny shadows will find you using other means of primitive direction finding.

WATCH IT

The sun is also used to figure direction with your watch. There are two methods; the "watch and stick" and the "hasty," both of which will determine direction, with the latter being less accurate.

The watch and stick is nearly as simple as the hasty, but more accurate. The primary advantage over the shadow stick method is time; you don't have to wait for the Earth to rotate on its axis and thus move the stick's shadow. Jam a meter-long stick into the ground so that it casts a shadow. Take your watch off your wrist and place it along the shadow so that the hour hand rests on the shadow pointing toward the stick. Now bisect the angle between the hour hand and 12 o'clock with an imaginary line. This line is a north-south line as opposed to a west-east line like that formed with the shadow stick method. South is in the direction formed by the imaginary line as it goes between the hour hand and noon.

If you are in the south temperate zone (23.4° south and 66.6° south), you must alter this method. Aim the noon hour at the stick along the shadow. Bisect the angle between it and the hour hand with an imaginary line. This is a north-south line, making north the direction of the imaginary line between noon and the hour hand.

Right now you should be asking yourself a question: Does this mean that the formula for the shadow stick method is different in the south temperate zone? Yes! When you place your feet at the objects marking the shadow tips, you are facing south. Now you're thinking.

The hasty method of using the watch to find the cardinal directions is simple; point the hour hand at the sun and bisect the angle between it and noon. This is due south in the north temperate zone (23.4° north and 66.6° north). In the south temperate zone, point the noon hour at the sun and bisect the angle with the hour hand.

So what if you have a digital watch? Easy. Draw a regular watch face on the ground and follow the procedure as if it were a real watch.

STRING AND STICK

Well before noon, jam that meter-long stick into the ground again so that a shadow is cast. Fix a length of string to the top of the stick which is long enough to reach a point on the ground about one foot from the base of the stick when held taut. Pivot the string around the stick to four equidistant spots, placing a shorter stick, rock, or whatever at each of these points. Draw a circle around the stick now using the markers as guides to keep the circle true. Where the shadow of the stick is touching the circle, place a second object.

As noon approaches, the shadow being cast by the stick will shorten, then lengthen as the noon hour passes and continues into afternoon. When the shadow once again touches the edge of the circle, place another object. Now draw a line between the two sets of double objects, and another line from the shadow stick so that it bisects the first line at a right angle. Stand behind the shadow stick with the sun at your back, picturing the imaginary line. You are facing north.

Right about here I think I had better explain something about the sun. Only on the equinoxes (somewhere very near March 21 and September 23) does it actually rise exactly in the east and set precisely in the west. The rest of the time it is off somewhat. At the sun's farthest point from the equinoxes it is farthest off course, so to speak. Mid-June sees Sol waking up to the northeast and dipping below the horizon to the northwest. In mid-September it rises in the southeast and heads back down in the southwest.

THE FLORA FACTOR

Vegetation (and how it grows) can be an indicator of direction but should never be considered a hard-and-fast rule of thumb.

One day in eastern Turkey (the country, not the town in North Carolina) I was sitting on a stump overlooking a distant bay. The region had been cut over many decades earlier. I was facing south and had a thought. In this hilly countryside, could I tell direction by the rings on the stumps? Vegetation tends to grow heaviest toward the south where it is generally warmer. I examined the rings of several stumps on this southern-facing gentle slope and found that they were markedly wider than on the northern side of the one-time trees. I took note of how wide the trees had been on the south side of the knoll and then walked over the crest to the north side. Here they were quite a bit wider and spaced farther apart. Trees on the south, sunny side grow thinner and are denser than on the cooler north side.

A few years ago I found myself in the Maritime Alps of southern France. This is glorious country, and the French-

Stump Rings Wider on South Side

men take good care of it. They love to hunt the wild European boar that make their home in the Alps, and most folks in this region know their way around nature. One day I was out hiking through the countryside and came across some boar hunters. Because I speak French, I took advantage of this opportunity to ask them about navigation in these rugged mountains. None of them had a compass, but one explained that a way of finding their way around was by observing the fallen trees. They told me that most trees up here fall with the prevailing wind, which in this range was usually out of the north. Sure enough, most of the trees that had fallen had done so to the south. They also used prominent peaks to terrain associate, and in periods of bad weather, which was common, they used the streams (they had a good grasp of the drainage pattern).

A TRIP THROUGH THE COSMOS

The rest of the stars are just as important—if not more so—in wayfinding as the sun, our nearest star. Ancient mariners like the Polynesians, Chinese, and Phoenicians all used the stars (celestial navigation) to cross the seas for purposes of trade or simply pure exploration. The Polynesians did so to establish new societies far from their ancestral homes. The stars are like road signs pointing to points unseen but there nonetheless. Once you have learned how to read them, wayfinding takes on a whole new meaning. And the feeling you get when accurately using the stars to navigate through regions of genuine wilderness, well, it is very gratifying to say the least. The sense of self-sufficiency you feel is both calming and reassuring.

Polaris
Polaris, also known as the North Star and the Pole Star, was identified thousands of years ago as a navigational constant. All other stars, as viewed from our planet in the northern hemisphere, revolve around Polaris. But there is a

common misconception about Polaris: many people wrongly believe that the North Star is always the brightest in the night sky. Uh-uh. Wrong. No. Incorrect.

Polaris is the last star in the handle of the Little Dipper (Ursa Minor), and it is anything but conspicuous. In fact, the whole of the Little Dipper is hard to see. It doesn't jump out at you when you stare up at the stars. It hides among a cluster of galactic neighbors many light years distant and takes a far backseat to its brother, the Big Dipper, a.k.a. Ursa Major, where brightness and size are concerned. Yet Polaris is the star that points to true (polar) north. Always.

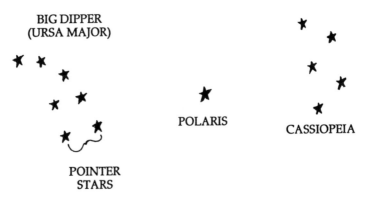

The Big Dipper, Polaris, and Cassiopeia

Well, since Polaris is so faint and obscure in the grand scheme of things, how do we find it?

We bracket. How do we bracket? *Bracketing is placing one object in between two others and using the relative distances between the three objects as reference points to locate or fix the primary.* In the case of Polaris, which you may not be able to pick out right away, you locate the Big Dipper among the other constellations. The Big Dipper rotates around Polaris just like all the other stars, so it will change its position in the night sky as the hours pass. It may not be visible as a whole or in part from time to time due to it being wholly or partially below the horizon. Remember that. The Big Dipper's scoop is constructed of four stars (the handle has three stars), the outer two of which are known as the pointer stars. Imagine a line being drawn from the bottom pointer star to the upper one, and continue it out along this axis for a distance of about five times that between the two pointers. At the end of this imaginary axis is the region where the North Star is located. But unless you know exactly what you are looking for, you may not be able to correctly identify which one it really is. So we bracket.

Continue looking along that imaginary axis another five times the distance between the pointers. You will come to a set of five fairly bright and obvious stars arranged in a lazy zig-zag fashion that may look like an "M," "E," "3," or "W," depending on what time of night you are looking for it. This constellation is named Cassiopeia. It forms the other half of the bracket. Now you have a reference. The North Star is half-way between Cassiopeia and the two pointer stars in Ursa Major. It sits pretty much smack dab in the middle of the two constellations with no other star obscuring its glow, though it doesn't shine like a beacon by any stretch of the imagination. The North Star is never more than 1° off true north.

Southern Cross

You haven't seen the stars until you have seen the Southern Cross shining in the night sky. I first saw this legendary constellation blazing in the inky blankness of a tropical night as we sailed past Australia's North West Cape toward the island of Bali in the Greater Sunda Islands. There was no mistaking it then, and there is no mistaking it now. It fires the nocturnal tropics in a blaze that has been written and spoken about for millennia.

The Southern Cross marks the South Pole as Polaris marks the North. However, it isn't precisely over due south. To find south from the Southern Cross, extend an imaginary line along the Cross' long axis a distance equal to five times the length of that long axis. From that point just look straight down toward the horizon. This is south.

If you are going to be wandering around in the boonies, you had better know how to take care of yourself. Wayfinding is only one skill that you will need to master. The business of survival is another. The following chapter is inextricably linked to the art of wayfinding and wilderness navigation.

CHAPTER EIGHT

SURVIVAL AND THE WAYFINDER

He was dead. As dead as you can get, I suppose, the merciless Mojave sun having cooked him good. Separated from his marine unit on the Corps' sprawling, evil-hot base at Twenty-Nine Palms, California, the young leatherneck never had a chance. He lacked any worthwhile desert survival training, and those responsible for him failed to account for him in a timely manner. It cost the young man his life. His body was found long after he disappeared one evening from his lonely outpost adjacent to the foreboding Bullion Range, a rumpled mass of near barren hills that have tested the mettle of many a man.

But his death was not without purpose. This graphic lesson has served to force thousands of men and women to take heed in the desert, and anywhere else where nature reigns supreme and uncontested. Had he only known how to use the stars to navigate, make a survival shelter out of his gear, find water in a dry streambed, recognize which plants were edible, signal a distant vehicle or aircraft, tend to his wounds, and build a fire using primitive means, the story would have turned out differently.

But for every grim tale there is one of hope and courage. Even against the most terrible odds, man and

Africa sports plenty of game for the wayfinder in need of food, but plenty of danger goes along with it.

woman come through to tell the tale of survival when all seemed lost. Jim and Jennifer Stolpa lost their way one winter afternoon in the northern Great Basin Desert after their vehicle became disabled. With them was their infant son. After trudging through the desert snows for many miles, Jim, a young soldier, stashed his wife and child in a tiny cave at the base of a bluff and walked nearly fifty miles without stopping, across a wilderness that has taken countless lives, until he came to a road where a passing driver stopped and helped him. Rescuers were alerted, and hours later they found his wife and baby, alive, in the remote cave. Jim and Jennifer lost some bone and tissue due to frostbite, but they survived, as did the baby. They had the will to survive, and when you've got that, there's nothin' gonna beat ya. It was like crossing the Saudi-Kuwaiti border that bleak, dreary morning in February 1991. We were going to win, and that was all there was to it. Jim and Jennifer were winners, too.

THE PATTERN FOR STAYING ALIVE

By virtue of their mission, the armed forces of the United States has a major stake in the survival game. There are four survival schools operated by the Department of Defense, located in Maine, North Carolina, California, and Washington. Each teaches a systematic method of wilderness survival known as The Pattern for Staying Alive. I am certainly not the originator of this system; no one individual is, though the name had to have been thought up by someone. But the name isn't important. What is important is the system, which has been taught at the schools for many years.

Many studies have been done on survival episodes. A bush pilot loses power over the Yukon and goes down. An experienced sailor has her boat sunk in the South Pacific. A sheep hunter loses his way in the Canadian Rockies. A little girl wanders away from her vacationing family in the Smokies. It can happen to any one of us, and does, with alarming frequency. Although every survival situation is different in many ways, all have several factors in common. These factors are what The Pattern is based upon. The aforementioned studies have shown that every survivor, regardless of the exact circumstances of the situation, faced at least one of seven threats to his or her existence. These threats are known as the Seven Enemies of Survival, and they are the factors responsible for the creation of The Pattern for Staying Alive.

The Pattern for Staying Alive, as taught at the U.S. Department of Defense Survival Schools, consists of five skill areas that you should be adept in, which are easily remembered by the formula:

FEW SURVIVORS FIND FAST SOLUTIONS

By taking the first letter of each word you can remember the five skill areas: First aid, Signals, Fire, Food and water, and Shelter. I prefer to add a sixth area, navigation, so you end up with:

FEW SURVIVORS FIND FAST SOLUTIONS NATURALLY

The Pattern defends against the Seven Enemies of Survival: Boredom and loneliness (thought of as one threat with two faces), Pain, Thirst, Fatigue, Temperature extremes, Hunger, and Fear. They are remembered by the formula:

BE PREPARED TO FACE THESE HOSTILE FACTORS

Each of these words' first letters equates to one of the Seven Enemies of Survival. Every survivor will face at least one of these threats, possibly more. The Pattern for Staying Alive solves for them all.

FIRST AID

Doctor who? Doctor you, that's who. If you are going to be traipsing around back o'beyond, then you are going to have to learn primitive medicine. You need not be an MD or paramedic to fix yourself or another in the wilderness in many cases. Obviously you are not going to be performing neurosurgery or transplanting any organs, but if you spend enough time in the wild places you are going to have medical problems. Guaranteed.

INJURIES TO THE BONES

There are two types of fractures: simple (closed) and compound (open). Both are serious, although the compound fracture is normally considered more severe due to the nature of the injury.

Simple fractures are those where the bone does not break through the covering muscle tissue or skin. Compound breaks are those where the bone tears through the muscle tissue and/or skin.

Symptoms: Pain, swelling, increased sensitivity, deformity, dysfunction, crepitus (when the sharp, opposing ends of the broken bone rub together, causing extreme pain and increasing the danger of secondary injury due to tissue or vascular damage), and discoloration.

Assessment: Take a close look at the injured area; remove any clothing necessary to see the site. Check for swelling, sensitivity, discoloration, temperature changes (cold), deformity, and loss of movement.

Treatment: Immobilize the bone from the first joints up and down from the fracture site and splint it. Treat for shock. Clean and dress the wound, and be sure to stop all bleeding. Elevate the wound to reduce swelling, and loosen restrictive clothing to allow for normal circulation. Check for additional injuries, too.

It is vital to keep a compound fracture clean. Infection far from professional medical services might just be fatal.

A dislocation occurs when the end of a bone is somehow pulled or twisted away from the joint it is supposed to be part of. The symptoms are similar to those of a simple fracture, as is the treatment.

SOFT TISSUE INJURIES

Soft tissue injuries include abrasions, contusions, punctures, blisters, avulsions (the tearing away of flesh), amputations, and crushes. The most common of these injuries in a wilderness setting are abrasions and contusions, followed by punctures, blisters, crushes, avulsions, and amputations. There is no way of telling which is going to happen to you or a member of your party; therefore, you must be prepared for any and all of them.

All of these injuries will fall into one of two categories: open or closed. Open soft tissue injuries show a break in the skin. Closed do not. Treating a closed injury is easier than fixing an open injury. Use the *R I C E* formula:

REST: This ensures that circulation doesn't impede the forming of clots via the heart functioning at an elevated rate.

ICE: As temperature decreases, blood vessel constriction increases, slowing bleeding. Wrap the ice in cloth and apply it to the wound using the 30/3/24-48 rule, which means apply the ice for approximately 30 minutes every 3 hours or so for a day or two.

COMPRESSION: Apply a pressure dressing (or use manual pressure) so that the bleeding stops but circulation to the wound site does not. Blood (oxygen) starvation of a wound and its surrounding tissue could result in amputation later on. If you can't feel a pulse distal to the wound (away from the heart), it is too tight. Check the dressing frequently to ensure that swelling hasn't tightened the dressing too much.

ELEVATE: Get that wound situated so that it is above the level of the victim's heart. This does two things; the pressure on the blood vessels is reduced, and the flow of blood to the affected area is decreased, thus reducing bleeding.

Never underestimate the severity of a closed soft tissue injury. Such mistakes have cost countless lives that need not have been lost.

Whereas contusions (bruises) and hematomas (pools of blood retained within the tissue) are closed wounds, open wounds consist not only of lacerations (cuts) and abrasions (scrapes), but punctures (such as those created by bullets, twigs in the eyes, etc.), crushes, avulsions, and amputations. Any of these can kill the victim in a shockingly short period of time if you fail to act quickly and correctly. Even comparatively minor wounds can cause shock. Shock kills.

Lacerations

The nature of the laceration will dictate if sutures (stitches) are indicated. Some cuts are straight, while others are jagged. The depth and location of the laceration have a lot to do with whether or not you start sewing. Also, lacerations are prone to infection and reopening if you aren't careful. Much more than skin can be damaged by a laceration. Blood vessels, tendons, ligaments, and organs can all be hurt.

Abrasions

An abrasion occurs when the skin is scraped or rubbed off. If you have ever fallen on pavement, you know what an abrasion feels like. Sometimes, depending on the nature of the injury, the wound may have small pieces of debris in it. You must clean it well to prevent infection. Capillary bleeding is common with abrasions and is easily stopped with direct pressure and elevation.

Punctures

Puncture wounds are very easily infected and can cause severe damage at the innermost extent of the wound. Internal bleeding from tissue, blood vessel, and organ damage is common. A puncture wound may show arterial bleeding (bright red blood—heavily oxygenated—that spurts with each beat of the heart), veinous bleeding (dark red blood that appears as a steady flow), or capillary bleeding. Unless the object that caused the puncture is interfering with breathing, leave it there if it's still in, no matter how bad it looks. It may be tamponading severed blood vessels, which means the object is actually preventing more serious bleeding. Removing it may cause profuse hemorrhaging. If at all possible wait for professional help.

Crushes

With crush wounds you have to consider more than meets the eye. The underlying organs and tissue, as well as blood vessels and bones, may be severely damaged. Internal bleeding is common in crush wounds, and if the abdominal region has been crushed, the liver may have been lacerated from broken ribs. Get that victim to a hospital fast.

Avulsions

When a section of skin ranging from a small piece to a part of a limb is torn off, you have an avulsion. If you can find it, place the avulsed material back where it came from and tape it into place, being sure to leave room for drainage. Minor avulsions may not need immediate further treatment, but major wounds will. Infection is always a concern with avulsions.

Amputations

A sudden traumatic amputation is life-threatening, even if the limb removed is a finger or toe. Quick action to stop the bleeding if it is profuse (some amputations show little bleeding) and treating for shock are key considerations. If possible, find the extremity or limb and save it, keeping it cool if you can. Limbs are regularly reattached nowadays. Just don't submerge the limb in ice so that it is in direct contact with it. This will likely cause frostbite and other cold injuries that adversely affect the reattachment process.

Blisters

Feet blisters are one of the most common wilderness injuries. They range from the proverbial hot spot, which may become a blister if not taken care of, to large blisters that impede movement. Prevention can solve this problem before it happens. Well broken-in footwear, two pair of quality socks, frequent rest stops to check your feet, and common sense all serve to prevent blisters. Spending an inordinate amount of time in the woods as I do, my feet are important to me, but sometimes I still get a blister or two. The worst case was a two-day force march across the Camp Lejeune Marine Corps base in North Carolina, and back again. I could barely walk for three days following the little jaunt because of tremendous blisters all over my feet. We weren't able to stop as often as we would have liked, and the boots used by the Corps at the time weren't exactly high-quality footwear, so we pressed on. The result was ugly indeed.

Large blisters should be drained and protected from further rubbing/friction and infection, but small blisters should just be protected, not drained.

INFECTIONS

Any open wound, regardless of the severity, can become infected. Symptoms include increased sensitivity at the site, swelling, reddened skin, pus, swelling, very noticeable heat radiating from the site, feverlike symptoms (alternating hot flashes and chills), obviously swollen lymph nodes, and red streaks coming out of the wound site.

Drain the wound if possible and treat it with 10-percent povidone-iodine. This is the solution we use at the Navy Survival School. Keep the wound clean and change the dressing frequently. Watch for signs of the infection spreading. Be prepared to evacuate the patient.

BODY FLUIDS AND DISEASES

If you become HIV positive, you are dead. With that in mind, let's take a quick look at how to prevent your dying from AIDS contracted through contaminated body fluids from an injury.

Your wilderness medical kit should contain latex gloves. Wear them when dealing with open wounds. A surgical mask placed over the nose and mouth and eye protection are also indicated. Blood and other body fluids can get into the provider's mouth, nose, or eyes. Never underestimate the AIDS threat. Never.

Also, tuberculosis is making a comeback in America due to treatment-resistant strains that have survived our medical onslaught. TB requires a six-month treatment program. You don't want that, now do you?

BLEEDING

Bleeding can be stopped in a number of ways. Direct pressure alone works well in most cases. Elevation of the wound above the level of the heart also works, as does using a pressure point (applying pressure to a blood vessel where it crosses over a bone near the surface of the skin), a constricting band a few inches above the wound that reduces blood flow, and as an absolute last resort, a tourniquet. Never release a tourniquet once it is applied. Leave that to the surgeon who is almost certainly going to amputate the limb.

ANIMAL-INFECTED WOUNDS

When this topic is brought up we usually think about snakes. But there are plenty of other little rascals out there that don't mind envenomating you. Spiders, scorpions, bees, wasps, hornets, chiggers, and ticks are just a few. Then you have marine envenomations from critters like jellyfish, Portuguese man-of-war, cone shells, stingrays, fire coral, and other sea creatures. Some of these animals' delivery mechanisms are purely defensive when dealing with humans (bees, wasps, hornets, stingrays, fire coral), some are offensive (chiggers and ticks), while others are both (spiders, scorpions, jellyfish, man-of-war, cone shells). As someone who spends time in out-of-the-way places, you may have to deal with some of these guys from time to time, and chances are it won't be pleasant if they decide to take a disliking to you.

Bees, Wasps, Hornets, and Ants (Hymenoptera)

No doubt you have heard about the evil killer bees, those hybrid Africanized honey bees that escaped from a facility in Brazil years ago and have now made their way north to you-know-where. Granted, they have attacked quite a few people between Texas and Brazil, but the chances of your being set upon by these ill-tempered little buggers is remote. What makes them so special is the undeniable fact that they have quick fuses, they will attack anything that they think is a threat to the hive en masse, and do so with considerable vigor. The venom they carry is potent, too. However, you stand a much better chance of having a memorable run-in with irritated wasps or the ever-popular yellow jackets, and there are dozens of species of other members of order Hymenoptera buzzing around the United States, too.

Some people are allergic to the venom of a bee. This life-threatening reaction, known as anaphylaxis or anaphylactic shock, must be treated with epinephrine immediately. Epinephrine is an antihistamine available through prescription. Every year in America approximately 100 people die as a result of anaphylaxis.

If you have been stung, remove the venom sack and attached stinger by scraping it off your skin. Clean the wound. If pain persists, use ice to reduce the swelling and take aspirin, ibuprofin, or acetaminophen.

Ants are members of Hymenoptera also. There are nearly 18,000 species of Hymenoptera in the United States, with well over 100,000 worldwide. The ant you really need to watch out for is, of course, the fire ant, which was accidentally imported to the United States in 1918. Now the South is literally infested with them, their telltale mounds adorning fields and pastures like land mines waiting for someone to step on them. If you have the ill-fortune to step or lie in a fire ant mound, you will soon come to understand why they have been so named. Get them off you.

As with any envenomation, prevention is your best bet. Some bees, hornets, and wasps live underground just like their cousins the ants. I once stepped right into a yellow jacket hive in Maine but had enough survival instinct to run for it as soon as the first swarm appeared from the burrow. I was lucky and didn't receive a single sting. Rich Hoffman, another instructor, wasn't so lucky after he committed the same crime. He was nailed repeatedly for his callousness but managed to survive the attack with no permanent harm done.

Arachnids

Many people believe spiders, scorpions, and ticks to be insects. They aren't. They are arachnids. Some are harmful to man, others aren't.

BROWN
RECLUSE
SPIDER

BLACK WIDOW
SPIDER

RED
HOURGLASS
FIGURE ON
UNDERSIDE OF
ABDOMEN

SCORPION

TICK

Arachnids

The only two spiders in America that you need worry about are the infamous black widow and the somewhat lesser known brown spider, a.k.a. brown recluse. The female black widow has the red hourglass-shaped marking on her abdomen. It doesn't like busy areas, preferring dark corners, woodpiles, and other such locales. I once saw a black widow pursue a child that had thrown a stick into her web (I was four at the time). It chased and caught him as he tried to clear a fence. He didn't think much of it until an hour later at the supper table when he spaced-out, began vomiting, and commenced to roll about the floor in what a friend of mine refers to as a "final, frenzied dance of death." Fortunately, they got him to a hospital and he lived. Other symptoms include abdominal rigidity (very common), nausea, and respiratory distress. The black widow's venom is primarily neurotoxic, and there is antivenin available. Therefore, deaths are uncommon though by no means unheard of. The American Red Cross says about half a dozen people die annually in the United States from black widow bites.

The brown spider is bad news. It lives in quiet places in the South and Midwest and uses a venom that attacks tissue. It is brown with a yellowish marking on its head that often appears violin-shaped. Flulike symptoms are common, but the bite may go unnoticed until the venom starts drastically acting on the wound site. Left untreated, the venom will form a necrotic ulcer (a large hole where the skin has died and rotted away). Get to a hospital after you clean the heck out of the wound.

According to Hollywood, the tarantula is a killer. This is only partly true, for the species found in America are almost completely harmless. So don't fret over American tarantulas. This is not true of species in the tropics.

Ticks are related to spiders and can be more dangerous. Some carry the well-known diseases Rocky Mountain Spotted Fever and Lyme Disease. Both are exceedingly dangerous maladies.

Ticks live in most of North America. They are not merely an annoyance; they are something you really want to avoid. Use a good insect repellent and check yourself frequently. If you find an attached tick, remove it with tweezers and clean the wound thoroughly. Grasp the tick as close to the skin as possible and avoid squishing it. If any unusual symptoms appear following a tick bite, seek medical help.

Scorpions are common in some of the warmer climes in North America, but deaths are rare. Only one species in the U.S. is considered potentially deadly, and then usually only to children and the elderly or infirm. If feverlike symptoms come on, see a doctor quickly. But for the most part, scorpions are only an annoyance.

Mosquitos carry many diseases, including malaria and yellow fever, as well as encephalitis. The best bet for prevention is covering body parts and using a repellent that is 100-percent DEET or close to it.

There exist in North America about 90,000 species of insects, with over 800,000 worldwide. Many are harmful to man in one way or another. Tsetse flies carry African sleeping sickness; house flies cholera, typhoid, and amebic dysentery. Horse flies carry anthrax, and sand flies a variety of tropical diseases. Blow flies carry cholera and typhoid, while deer flies carry diseases that strike the eyes. Fleas are vectors (carriers) of epidemic typhus and plague. Cockroaches carry an array of pathogens. Kissing bugs transmit Chagas' disease (New World sleeping sickness); lice transmit dermatosis and other ailments. So the potential for problems is certainly out there.

Snakes
The subject of poisonous snakebites is one that has been covered in many a book and magazine article. Treatments have changed over the years, and we now know more about these reptiles than we did 50 years ago.

There are four kinds of poisonous snakes in North America: rattlesnakes, copperheads, coral snakes, and cottonmouths (also known as cottonmouth water moccasins). Though all have taken lives, we only see about a dozen deaths from snakebites each year. Worldwide there are always in excess of 50,000 fatalities from snakebites annually, so we don't have it that bad.

What is the most dangerous snake in North America? That depends on what you mean by dangerous. Ounce for ounce, the venom of the Mojave rattler (*Crotalus scutulatus*) of the American Southwest wins. He hangs out in the desert and can be found at elevations of up to 5,000 feet. But bites from this character are rare when compared to bites from the eastern and western diamondback rattlers. They are found around man much more and have a bad attitude to boot. They sport hemotoxic venom as do most rattlers, cottonmouths, and copperheads. Coral snakes have a neurotoxic venom.

With only a dozen or so deaths per year from bad snakes in this country, why should you be concerned with them? Because about 8,000 bites are delivered by poisonous snakes, that's why. In the world? No, in America. Now you see my point.

The only three states in the United States that don't have any species of poisonous snakes are Hawaii, Alaska, and Maine. Some reference books claim that Maine has the timber rattler. No, it doesn't, and I defy anyone to find one in Maine. They aren't there, but early herpetologists thought they must be since they are documented in neighboring New Hampshire. They were wrong.

There are 14 or so species of rattlers in North America, four species of copperheads, one species of cottonmouth, and two species of coral snakes. Copperhead bites are quite common but usually aren't fatal since the venom is weak. The cottonmouth is nasty, but deaths are also uncommon. Coral snakes are comparatively docile and have relatively poorly developed fangs, but the toxin is bad. All rattlers are mean as far as I'm concerned.

There are far more species of poisonous snakes outside

North America. Many are aggressive and should be avoided at all costs. Quite a few are deadly to the point where treatment might be futile. The king cobra's bite is guaranteed to kill you unless you receive immediate treatment, and then it still may be too late. I had an altercation with an Egyptian cobra in the Middle East, and I didn't even do anything. An eight-footer sprinted across the road I was traveling down, so I stopped about 15 meters from it to let it go by. It saw me stop, so it stopped and reared up, flaring its hood and hissing bad snake words at me. I took off at warp speed and never looked back. No snake in the world can catch a marine when he's scared.

If the common krait, mamba, or tiger snake (Australia's answer to the king cobra) gets you, kill the snake before you die. At least you won't go alone.

Remember the old adage about slicing the fang holes, and then sucking the venom out with your mouth? Bad idea. Not only are you going to bleed, but the venom you suck out can be absorbed through the tissue below the tongue. Not good. Instead, immediately place a constricting band a few inches above the wound. Clean and disinfect it, and keep the wound below the level of the heart. Treat for shock, and use a fairly new device called the Sawyer Extractor to get the venom out. Buy one at a camping store and keep it in your kit. It is the best thing on the market.

Watch where you step and put your hands. Don't panic if bitten. Use your skills and keep your head about you. You stand an excellent chance of surviving.

Nonpoisonous snakebites are five to six times more common than poisonous snakebites. After all, there are many more species of nonpoisonous snakes around. So, if bitten by one, clean and dress the wound thoroughly, or you may get tetanus. Tetanus isn't funny.

Marine Envenomations

These include any bite or sting by a sea creature by

which venom is introduced into the body. Some are annoying, some are deadly.

Stingrays are a pain. They lie in the sand and wait for fish to swim by, which they pounce on. Their tails have a sharp, venomous barb filled with a protein-based neurotoxin that can cause extreme pain and in some cases death from anaphylaxis. Remove the barb and soak the wound in water as hot as you can stand. Heat destroys the protein.

I have been stung by the pesky Portuguese man-of-war more times than I care to remember. Their long tentacles have a surfeit of stinging cells called nematocysts which fire when touched and can sometimes cause severe anaphylaxis. They live mostly in tropical and subtropical seas, floating with the wind, waves, and tides. They are not jellyfish, but rather colonial hydroids. Remove the tentacle(s) and wash the area with salt water (fresh water will cause all the nematocysts to fire instantly and simultaneously). Then rinse the wound site with a 10-percent solution of ammonia and salt water.

Treatment for jellyfish stings is the same. The lion's mane jellyfish is one of the most dangerous in the world.

Some fish have poisonous barbs in their fins. The zebra fish and stonefish are two of these. If bitten, get a doctor.

Cone shells are carnivorous snails that have a poison dart they thrust into their victims. Some can be very deadly. The California cone is just one of many you need to avoid.

Sea snakes are true reptiles and all are poisonous, but your chances of being bitten by one are microscopic.

SHOCK

Shock can be thought of as the mind's inability to accept and handle what has happened to it, i.e., trauma of some kind. It manifests itself by shutting down the three parts of the body's circulatory system: the heart, blood vessels, and blood itself. Shock can strike a victim of a comparatively minor wound and turn the situation into something far more serious, even fatal. Failure to treat for shock may result in death from what was otherwise a nonfatal wound.

Symptoms: Rapid, fluttering, or weak pulse. Unusual thirst. Nausea, shallow and/or rapid respiration, and cool, pale, clammy skin. Also, dilated pupils, anxiety, and consciousness fluctuations.

Assessment: Shock normally manifests itself in more than one of these symptoms, but it does occasionally show up in singular fashion. Watch for them all. Anticipate, but don't create symptoms.

Treatment: Treatment goes right back to the very basics of first aid. Maintain an open airway, ensure that the victim is breathing, and check the circulation constantly. Start CPR if necessary.

Beyond this advice, keep the victim hydrated, elevate the legs to keep the blood in the major organs and reduce stress on the heart. Tend to other wounds as soon as possible and keep the victim warm.

Shock kills untold numbers of people every year. Don't underestimate it. Ever.

ALTITUDE MALADIES

People who venture above 8,000 feet on the ground are at risk of altitude maladies caused by oxygen deprivation. The body takes time to adapt to lowered barometric pressure, and when you go above 8,000 feet without allowing the body to adapt, things can go wrong.

Acute Mountain Sickness (AMS)

This most often strikes people who do not acclimatize and bolt straight to altitudes in excess of 8,000 feet.

Symptoms: Off-the-scale headache. Nausea and vomiting. Cyanosis (bluish or purplish discoloration of the skin as a result of oxygen deprivation), peripheral edema (swelling in the arms and legs), and a feeling of listlessness. Also, fitful sleep and a marked decline in appetite.

Assessment: Look for symptoms in those who do not wait to acclimatize and also those who partially do so and then make a jump to altitude. Symptoms may come in groups or singly.

Treatment: Drink water until you almost burst. Limit your activity for the first few days at altitude; rest frequently. Take the standard headache remedies if the headache persists. Descend to the altitude at which the symptoms first appeared if they start to become more serious.

High Altitude Pulmonary Edema (HAPE)

When fluid begins to pool in the lungs at altitudes over 8,000 feet (rarely lower), you get HAPE. This is a serious illness.

Symptoms: Along with symptoms of AMS, HAPE shows unusual fatigue and shortness of breath, along with an increase in respirations and heart rate. A cough often starts, and it may bring up phlegm. You can hear fluid in the lungs, even without a stethoscope (rales). Muscles may become markedly uncoordinated (ataxia).

Assessment: Be alert and watch for signs that progress from AMS. Check the fingernail beds for cyanosis. Blood in the sputum is an indicator, as is extreme lethargy. The face may also become cyanotic. The victim may lapse into unconsciousness.

Treatment: Immediately descend below the point where symptoms began. Treat for shock, and give oxygen if you have it available.

High Altitude Cerebral Edema (HACE)

This life-threatening illness normally occurs at an altitude of at least 10,000 feet, usually a little higher. The brain begins to swell, probably from hypoxia—or at least this is what doctors speculate, though the true cause is not proven.

    Symptoms: AMS and HAPE symptoms likely, plus seizures, partial or whole paralysis, hallucinations, inability to focus vision.

    Assessment: Be on guard for an array of the above symptoms.

    Treatment: Pay attention now. *Descend now!* Any questions? Treat for shock along the way. Don't screw around with HACE.

Perhaps you noticed that one common treatment in all the aforementioned illnesses resulting from altitude is to descend. You can't go wrong by descending, and it is the only sure-fire treatment.

HEAT INJURIES

As I write this, the temperature outside is 97°F, and the heat index makes it more like 115°F, according to the Weather Channel. I spent the morning playing with my rifle out on the range, where I put the first round into the black just after sunrise, spent an hour shooting there (at the 200 yard line), half an hour at the 300 yard line, and half an hour at the 500 yard line. By the time I finished I was drenched in sweat, and it was barely mid-morning. I drank a quart of water during that time but could still feel the first twinges of a dehydration headache coming on, so I gulped Gatorade until I couldn't drink any more. At 10:00 A.M. I did my abdominal exercises and ran several 100 yard dashes, but my time was off by more than a second. I felt drained, spent. The heat was robbing me despite all my precautions. I knew enough to shower up and drink some more water, calling it a day.

    You don't need to be in a desert to become a heat casualty. The summer of 1993 saw record high temperatures

across much of the eastern United States, with several people dropping dead due to the murderous heat, especially in
Philadelphia. Even the cows couldn't take it, their milk pro-
duction falling off drastically. The murder rate went up in
the cities, as it always does when the heat makes people
cranky. Emergency rooms overflowed with victims of heat
exhaustion and heat stroke.

What Makes a Heat Casualty?

This is a complex equation, but it is sometimes one that
is almost predictable. Once you have been a heat casualty
you are at increased risk of becoming one again. This is
called an acquired predisposition. Other factors that bring
on heat problems are the body's inability to compensate
for an increase in heat output, insufficient water intake
and storage, alcohol use (alcohol is a diuretic; it makes
you urinate), poor health, advanced age, overexertion
and lack of sleep, medication use, and a deficient salt
level in the body. When two or more of these factors
occur, trouble is afoot.

Heat Cramps

One of the worst cases of heat cramps I have witnessed
was while I was training lifeguards in San Diego. We
were running a summer course at a pool on Coronado, so
it was plenty hot with a dry Santa Ana wind blowing. A
strenuous morning of rescues was followed by a long-dis-
tance swim in the afternoon. The student hadn't con-
sumed enough water or salt, and his right calf muscle
paid for it. He let out a yelp and grabbed the side of the
pool, grimacing in what was obviously terrible pain. His
entire face was contorted in agony.

I pulled him up onto the deck and looked down at
his calf. It was rock hard. I applied an old massage trick
and released the cramp, but I knew that it was bound to
happen again soon if he didn't get some salt and water
into him. We did, and it didn't.

Symptoms: Sudden, severe, often debilitating muscle cramps that occur during or after exercise.

Assessment: Watch for crippling abdominal, thigh, and calf cramps (rarely in the feet, but when they strike here it is very painful). Acquired predisposition common.

Treatment: *Do not give salt tablets.* Instead, have the victim drink salt water (one-quarter teaspoon per quart of cool water) slowly. Lay the victim on his back with the legs elevated about six inches. Avoid further exercise that day. Drink Gatorade or some other quality sports drink that has salt, electrolytes, and other goodies in it. Drink plenty of them, too.

Heat Syncope

This is a fancy term for fainting caused by standing still in the heat for too long. I won't bother you with the exact medical terminology. I see this on a very regular basis when marines stand in a pre-parade formation for long periods in the hot Carolina sun. We sit in the shaded stands and take bets on how many are going to "turf dive" before the show is over. I usually win. What's better, only the corpsman (a navy witch doctor attached to the marines) is allowed to treat the marine, so the rest of the "jarheads" just stand there and giggle quietly. Yeah, we're weird.

Symptoms: Well, the victim faints after standing in the heat for too long with minimal movement.

Assessment: Once in a while the victim will teeter a little before falling or actually say that he or she feels funny, weak, or sick. Sometimes "dizzy" is used. The victim may or may not sweat profusely just before collapsing. Always look for injuries caused by the fall. Broken teeth, noses, and jaws are not uncommon. My friend

Bryan McCoy, who once commanded a company of marines at the U.S. Marine Barracks in Washington, D.C., saw a pal of his go down the hard way one day—straight into the pavement. He lost teeth and a lot of dignity. Bryan still laughs at that memory.

Treatment: The same as with heat cramps, but skip the salt water cocktail.

Heat Exhaustion

Now we are really getting serious. Heat exhaustion is often observed just before the onset of heat stroke, which can be fatal. However, this is not always the case. Some heat stroke victims never show signs of heat exhaustion. You must treat both as the serious illnesses they are. Never take either of these lightly.

Symptoms: Cool, sweaty, clammy skin. Nausea may be accompanied by the urge to vomit or dry heave. A feeling of dizziness, bad headache, and a feeling of weakness are common. The body temperature will increase by three or four degrees.

Assessment: This is a malady that you can often see coming, as the symptoms are classical and also point to dehydration. It is common for the victim to complain. Immediate treatment is the answer.

Treatment: Remove the victim from the causative environment, and get him or her into a cool one. This might mean spraying with water from a hose, submerging the torso in cool water if that is all that is available, and so on. But get the victim out of the heat! Remove fully all clothing, and have the victim rest on his back and drink cool water. Use a branch, clothing, or whatever to fan the victim (use the wind chill factor to his benefit).

Maintain a close watch on the symptoms and especially the core temperature.

Heat Stroke

Heat stroke can kill you deader than Hoffa. With that in mind, let's look at symptoms.

Symptoms: Red, dry skin (may progress to this from heat exhaustion left untreated). The respiration and pulse rate will elevate. If the victim is conscious he or she may become delirious. A comalike state is not uncommon for those who collapse. The core temperature will shoot above 104°F.

Assessment: This is a fairly easy one to assess, given the symptoms. The environment and activity of the victim are additional signs that heat stroke is the culprit.

Treatment: Be aggressive! Waffling on this one is not good, folks. Treat conscious victims the same as for heat exhaustion. Do not try to administer liquids to an unconscious victim. Get the victim to an emergency room fast. This is a killer.

As with most wilderness injuries, heat illnesses are preventable. Be proactive and stop them from happening. Watch for the early signs and don't let vanity sway you from acting.

COLD WEATHER CASUALTIES

Man is a tropical animal, meaning that he can only survive naked year-round in the tropics. However, because we are so darn smart, we have adapted to far different environments. We hang out on both Poles, fool around in outer space, find ways to get to some very deep spots in the oceans, and plant flags on the highest peaks. For a tropical animal, man sure likes cold places.

We've managed to find ways to stay warm in these places of extremes. But man also finds ways to injure and kill himself by not paying attention to the hostile environment he is in. Well, to tell you the truth, I have never considered the environment hostile. It is neutral, passive. The environment doesn't care what happens to you and doesn't go out of its way to make you happy or sad. But man perceives the environment as being hostile when things don't go his way.

And man goes out of his way to be cold. Robert Scott perished trying to beat Roald Amundsen to the South Pole in 1911, just so one could claim to be the first man to set foot on that spot. Every winter wild n' woolly mushers drive their dog teams across a large portion of Alaska to see who can go the distance in the shortest period of time. Mountaineers ply the Himalayas in search of the ultimate ascent. What is this fascination with the cold?

Whatever it is, it means that the cold is going to have an endless series of opportunities to injure man in his quests for glory and adventure. But like heat injuries, cold injuries are preventable.

Hypothermia

Hypothermia is a sustained cooling of the body's core temperature to 95F or below. It can happen in Florida, California, Washington, Maine, and every state in between. In fact, under the right circumstances, it can even occur in the tropics. Like heat exhaustion and heat stroke, hypothermia requires immediate attention. Failure to treat a hypothermic individual quickly and efficiently may result in death.

The body loses heat through four ways: evaporation, radiation, conduction, and convection. When these rascals gang up—and with the weather, activities of the victim, and other factors joining in—hypothermia strikes.

Evaporation in this case refers to sweat evaporating from the body in an attempt to cool it. When it goes too far, you have a problem. Radiation is your body heat being lost to the cold air or water, or both. Conduction is similar but requires direct contact between the skin and a cold material or object. Convection involves air or water moving over the skin and cooling it that way.

Symptoms: Shivering is your body's first natural defense against the cold. It will stop as hypothermia progresses. Hypothermia victims are sluggish and uncooperative quite often. They may not appear very concerned about the cold or their condition. They frequently become uncoordinated, and will stumble about if moving. Their speech pattern starts to go haywire, and their ability to think rationally goes down the tubes. If they are dehydrated as well, their urine will be dark.

Assessment: Be on the lookout for several symptoms to appear at once, which follow shivering. The mental faculties are often the first to go, but sometimes you will note physical manifestations first or at the same time. If the skin is unusually cold to the touch and the victim doesn't respond to questions or conversation normally, you are looking at a hypothermia victim in many cases.

Treatment: *Be aggressive!* As with heat exhaustion and heat stroke, get the victim out of the causative environment whenever feasible. Remove clothes that are sweat-soaked (common in hypothermia victims that have been skiing, snowshoeing, etc.), and dry the skin. Replace with warm, dry clothes. Get a wool hat on their heads. Give warm, sweet drinks to conscious victims (no caffeine; we don't want the urine output to increase), and rewarm them near a fire, in a cabin, vehicle, etc. You may have to get naked with the victim in a dry sleeping bag or other arrangement; a warm body against a cold body is a tried and true survival trick. *No alcohol!* It dilates the blood vessels and increases heat loss. You may need to perform CPR in particularly severe cases. Don't let the victim get cold again. Treat for shock, too.

One of the least expected (I was thinking about other things at the time, like being blown up or shot in the head) hypothermia cases I have ever encountered was in the northern Arabian Desert. We were in a very leaky shelter, and it had been raining nonstop for three days in the surprisingly frigid Arabian winter. I noticed that one of my men—a corpsman, of all things—hadn't moved from his hunched-over position in about two hours. I thought he was reading a book but he wasn't. I approached him from behind and tapped him on the shoulder. No response. "Doc," I said. Nothing. "Hey, Doc!" I yelled. Nada. Oh-oh.

I walked around in front of him and got the classic thousand-yard stare. He was soaked to the bone and quite hypothermic. Half an hour later I had him "good to go" as they say, having gotten his wet clothes off, a lot of hot cocoa into him, and so on and so on. Hypothermia in Arabia! (I later beat him for scaring me like that.)

Frostbite

Genuine frostbite is frozen tissue—not cool or cold tissue—but frozen tissue, usually in the extremities such as fingers and toes, plus ears and the nose, where capillary action isn't so good in the first place. It is easy to detect.

Symptoms: Minor frostbite presents a hard whitish or grayish patch of skin that is soft on the underside. When treated (rewarmed), blisters appear no more than a day afterward. Deep frostbite looks the same as minor frostbite, but the patch is hard from top to bottom. This means that more than a few layers of skin have been frozen. It means that the entire depth of skin and possibly muscle tissue beneath the skin has been frozen.

Assessment: When the cold is amplified by wind or water (or both), be alert for signs on the extremities.

Treatment: Thaw the entire site by submerging it in warm water at about 102°-108°F. Do not allow it to become refrozen. Keep the wound elevated and well-dressed. Ensure that circulation is unhindered. Be ready for extreme pain as it thaws. In bad cases watch for shock. Get medical help.

There are countless other medical malfunctions I could go into here but to do so would turn this book into a medical manual, which it was never meant to be. Suffice it to say that if you are going to be peregrinating in the backcountry, you had better have more than a basic first-aid course under your belt.

EMERGENCY SIGNALS

My brother-in-law Nick, an upper-management honcho for a large corporation, showed me a test that dealt with decision-making and group dynamics that was given to some of his firm's management. It contained a list of survival items that a group had available after their plane went down in the desert in the summer. They had to prioritize what to save and what to discard. At the top of the list was a signal mirror. What?! Not water? No, water was second, I believe. In this particular situation the mirror was definitely the best first choice.

There are two categories of signal: audio and visual. A signal plan must take both into account. A signal plan must be ready for effective use at all times, be diversified, and able to be put into effect during all weather conditions.

Audio Signals

You have of course heard that three gun shots fired rapidly, one immediately after the other, is an SOS signal.

(Three shots could also mean that a nearby hunter needs to improve his aim.) But one signal is not a signal plan, and three gun shots may not do the trick.

A sturdy, plastic whistle (not a metal one, which could freeze to your lips in cold weather) belongs in every signal kit. Banging metal on metal, or striking any hard object against another is a good audio signal. So, too, is the human voice. A yell down a valley on a cloudy day might be heard for miles. Use whatever you can; improvise.

Visual Signals

As with audio signals, visual signals are limited only by your imagination insofar as concepts are concerned. Man can see farther than he can hear in most circumstances, however, and this means that visual signals are used to effect a rescue more often than audio signals. (But this does not mean that you should ignore audio signals! The principle of the foghorn serves well to prove that audio signals are just as important in your signal plan as visual ones.)

When I was going through training to become a wilderness survival instructor, one of the men who showed me a thing or two was John Lamanna, a Navy Seabee who was on an instructor tour at the school in western Maine. One day John constructed a smoke signal on a triangular platform a few feet off the ground. Into this triangle he wove fir and spruce boughs around a thick pile of paper birch bark. He lit the strip of birch bark he had left hanging out from the base of the fir and spruce boughs and stepped back. Within seconds the green boughs were producing an astonishing amount of smoke that could be seen for miles. It burned for a solid 10 minutes before showing any signs of slowing down. Such a visual signal can be a lifesaver, and it took only half an hour to build from start to finish.

Besides smoke, fire itself has been used as an emergency signal more times than we will ever know. Three signal fire sets that are prepared to be lit at a moment's notice, set in a triangular pattern at least ten meters apart, will tell most anyone that someone has a problem. The same is true for smoke signals during the day. However, with the latter, arrange them in a linear fashion on the downwind side of a clearing if you expect that clearing may be used as a helicopter landing zone. You don't want smoke blowing across the zone and obscuring the pilot's vision.

The signal mirror is great. Under optimal conditions its flash can be seen for dozens of miles. When you see what you want to hit with the flash, raise your free-hand fingertips to a point where they are resting "on" the object, then manipulate the mirror in your other hand until the flash strikes the fingertips. It would be nice if the sun were always situated in front of you so that the flash could easily strike the plane, boat, helicopter, or what have you, but this is rarely the case, it seems. However, even with the sun behind you—yes, behind you—the signal mirror can still be used quite well. Just lie down on your back with the mirror in your hand behind your head with the arm stretched out. The other hand is your aiming point as before. The lower the sun in the sky, the flatter the mirror should be to the ground as you hold and manipulate it.

Do not aim the flash at the cockpit of an aircraft, as this could temporarily blind the pilot if he is close. Aim at the fuselage.

Polished metal can be used as a stand-in for a real mirror.

Any material that contrasts with the background can be used as a signal. Seaweed arranged in an SOS pattern on the beach, dark logs or heavy branches arranged in a light-colored field, brightly colored cloth or aviation air panels, and literally any other such system can be used.

There are several makes and models of flares and flare guns on the market. The compact pen or pencil flare is popular, but some shoot higher and burn brighter and longer than others. Select the best one available. Don't skimp. My friend George Misko, an interrogator/translator, recently found out the hard way about these cheap flares. The boat he was in conked out off a North Carolina beach at dusk, and the wind and wave action started pushing the boat toward the surf zone, which was something he was hoping to avoid. A helicopter flying nearby didn't see the small flare he shot into the air, as it burned only for a few seconds, and by the time he had reloaded, the chopper was gone. He was about to ignite a seat cushion and set it in the water when his partner got the motor going.

FIRE

Few people think of fire as a chemical reaction, but it is one of the greatest chemical reactions we humans have learned to exploit. There is no telling how man first learned to create fire, though he almost certainly first saw and contemplated fire that had been created by lightning. But he has been using it for tens of thousands of years and with good reason. Fire has multiple uses in a survival situation.

Fire cooks food, which often tastes better and is usually safer to eat when cooked. Fire keeps us warm when we are freezing to death and provides company when we are lonely. It can sterilize a knife you are about to use to lance a boil, boil water for a cup of tea, signal a would-be rescuer, keep the wild critters at bay (if you really think those coyotes are after you, which they are not), and fills in nicely for the TV you miss so much (plus it has countless channels and never shows reruns).

The Fire Triangle

Since fire is a chemical reaction, it must have certain ingredients in order to work. These are heat, oxygen (air), and fuel. All three factors must be present and in proper proporptions for a fire to appear. Two of these will not make a fire without the third. It's all or nothing.

Getting It Going

Creating a fire in the wilderness under less than perfect conditions is an art steeped in lore. It can be a frustrating experience if you don't know what you are doing. If you're good, you can start a fire in a flooded wind tunnel. If you're not, well . . .

Start by selecting and preparing the fire site. This is a crucial first step. The right fire will never occupy the wrong site. Never. Select a spot that is out of the wind but which has air circulation such as a light breeze. It should be within a few minutes' walk of fuel sources, be safe so that it doesn't lend itself to getting out of control, and be situated near your camp. Clear all the peripheral ignitables away from the edges. Don't set a ring of rocks around the edge. If you clear away the peripheral ignitables, you won't need rocks, which have a tendency to explode when superheated if they have a certain moisture content. Exploding rocks are not amusing when you are in the line of fire.

Gather all the tinder, kindling, and fuel you will need. Tinder is what you start with, that bone dry grass, yellow or paper birch bark, dead conifer needles, or other material that bursts into flame when struck with a spark or tiny flame. You could use the lint from your pockets or navel, cotton or wool fibers pulled from clothing, steel wool fibers, cotton balls from your survival kit (which you can treat with petroleum jelly to make even better tinder), the downy seed heads from a cattail, etc. Kindling is dry twigs, wood shavings, sticks, punk wood (the dry core of rotten logs), and so on. This is applied only after you get the tinder going well, being sure not to smother it. Take your time. After the kindling is going well, apply the fuel level of combustible material. This is stuff like sections of limbs, logs, and other heavy fuel that will burn even when a little damp.

Types of Fires

Design your fire with a purpose in mind. A teepee fire is a basic design good for quick warming and light cooking, as well as signaling. A log cabin fire is designed for maximum heat and burns for a long time. It is a good cooking fire, too. The pyramid fire will collapse onto itself and make a nice bed of coals that will keep you warm throughout the night. The coals can be dug through in the morning to get your fire going again without using another match or your lighter. A star fire is a small fire made of several sticks or small limbs and is good for when a limited amount of kindling is available. The trench fire is useful in windy conditions, as it keeps the base of the fire below ground level. A lean-to fire uses a green log as a side base and has multiple uses. There are many other designs, far too many to go into here. Experiment and use the one that best suits the situation.

Your fire kit should contain at least three ignition devices. Some examples would be a magnesium block with striker (available in many camping stores), a metal match (also available in camping stores), wooden "strike any-where" kitchen matches in a waterproof container, butane lighters, hurricane matches (available in outdoor catalogs), or a Zippo lighter with fresh fluid. Also included in your fire kit should be a variety of tinder and kindling. Such material is available in camping stores.

You must practice to be a good fire starter and builder in all weather conditions with a variety of materials. Get out there in the rain and try it one night, without the aid of a flashlight, either. Be hard on yourself; it doesn't come overnight. The time may come when your fire-building skills mean life or death.

FOOD AND WATER

The human body is made up largely of fluids. This, and the fact that most survival situations are safely ended in less than 24 hours, means that water is usually more important to the survivor than is food. Obviously, in a long-term survival predicament, food will be very important as well, but such situations are uncommon. On the other hand, in a 7-10 day survival situation, food could make a tremendous difference in how it all turns out.

But water is our life source. I had a professor in college who touted the party line about life on Earth having originated in some slimy sea of primordial ooze a bizillion years ago, or some such thing. This could be true for all I know, but since I wasn't around at the time, I'll never really know for sure. But no matter where we Earthlings came from so long ago, the fact remains that water is vital to our continued existence, both as individuals, and as a species. We must have water.

Clouds obscure terrain features, even in the Mohave Desert.

Finding Water While Wayfinding

I have found water in many places I haven't exactly expected it, primarily in deserts. I spent most of January and February of 1993 in California's Mojave Desert. It rained so

Dry arroyos carry flash floods that take lives every year.

much that huge intermittent lakes formed in the basins, and the arroyos raged with frothing torrents of brown, muddy

123

water. In the Arabian Desert it frequently rained on us during the winter months, and the Kuwaiti spring bestowed bone-jarring thunderstorms and electrical displays like I had never seen before and may not see again. For places that are supposed to be dry as a sidewinder's belly, there sure is a lot of rain in the desert.

There are so many ways to find (or make) water that I hardly know where to begin. But I'll give it a shot.

First, get out your map and look for some. "Duh," you say? Hey, you would be amazed at how many people don't think to look at their topographic map for water. It's easy to find the lakes, ponds, rivers, streams, and other obvious watering holes. But the more subtle indicators are another matter. Think about gravity. Water runs downhill, right? The base of that cliff or rock outcropping could have a pool of water or tiny stream. Your map may not show any water in a certain draw, but it still may be there. Springs don't always show up on topo maps, either. That intermittent streamed may be dry on the surface in

This intermittent lake will disappear in the summer months.

the dead of summer but underneath is water. Dig down along the outside of bends—three feet will often suffice.

Where two animal trails converge, follow the single one they form. It may very well lead to water. A crevice or crack in a rock outcropping that is lined with bird, frog, or toad droppings means that water is at the base of the crack. Siphon it out with the long piece of surgical tubing you carry in your survival kit. Birds drink regularly at dawn and dusk; watch their flight patterns. Seeing doves all heading in one direction at dawn and dusk is a sure sign that water lies in that direction.

On the Great Plains, pronghorns are never far from water. Follow them very discreetly from a distance, and they'll lead you to water within a few hours or so. In Nevada and Utah, wild horses still exist. Follow them to water when they are all walking in a straight line and not meandering around. They are probably heading for the proverbial watering hole.

Transpiration Bag

Vegetation Bag/Still

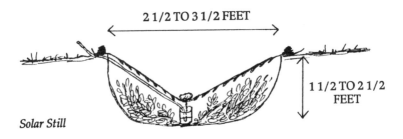

Solar Still

Listen for frogs and toads at night. They sit in water and sing to each other.

Plants tell of water, too. Willow trees mean water, and they often can be seen from miles away lining a hidden stream or creek. Some cacti hold prodigious amounts of water (barrel, pincushion, cereus, prickly pear), while others have water that tastes too bad to drink. Coconuts hold water, but they have a mild laxative effect so don't overindulge.

You can make water, too. The illustrations above and on the previous page of the transpiration bag, vegetation still, and solar still tell it all. You can also wrap an absorbent cloth around your ankles and walk in the dew-covered grass early in the morning or after a rain. You can set out containers to catch rain water running off plants and rocks. If one of those plants is a vine, slice it at top and bottom and catch water running out the lower end. On the beach, dig a pit behind the first dune (no matter how low the dune is) about three feet deep. Let the water seep into the shored-up hole and let it settle for a few hours. The top two inches or so are potable.

Now, if you can't find water after all that, then somebody obviously has it in for you.

Cultural food biases must be ignored in a survival situation.

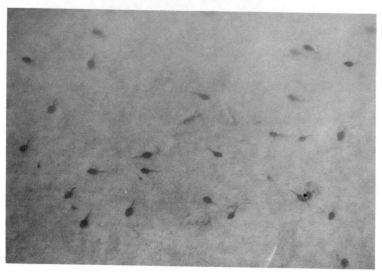

Tadpoles can be included in a stew or used as bait.

This jackrabbit may not taste great but it is food.

Lizards come in all shapes and sizes and are edible.

Wading birds are easy to snare and can be quite large—just make sure you are in a bonafide survival situation.

The right fishing hole means plenty of food for the wilderness wayfinder.

Approaching prairie dogs require stealth.

Deer often herd up when browsing.

White-tailed deer are creatures of habit. This means you can hunt or snare them.

This crow was lured in by a grape thrown on the ground.

This rabbit fell to a burrow snare.

Finding Food While Wayfinding

Few places on the spinning orb we call home have no food whatsoever for us to dine upon. Even the tops of the highest Antarctic mountain have lichens growing on the rocks, though you would be hard-pressed to get at them and find enough to make a difference. Very hard-pressed, indeed. But the point is that food is almost everywhere. It's only a matter of finding it and rendering it edible.

Cultural food biases are something the survivor can't afford to have. I have practiced eating things that my culture says are taboo, simply because I want to get over those biases in case I end up in an out-of-the way spot where my wife Susan's broccoli casserole, my mother's roast beef with Yorkshire pudding, and my own Mexicali moose aren't on the menu. I've tried roasted bamboo bats (good), steamed eel (also good), live minnows (not so good), and a variety of other taste treats and urge you to do the same.

The wilderness wayfinder who is also a survivor enduring a long-term situation where food acquisition is a must should take special pains to vary his diet. One food isn't going to get it. You must strive to get a balanced meal as often as possible, and this means that hunting and gathering are going to come into play. With plants you don't know, you are going to have to run a taste test on them before eating.

Before doing a taste test, make sure that there is enough of the plant in the area to make it worthwhile. Check the plant to see if it has insects; has white, milky sap; thorns; hairy fibers; or other features that you don't want. Break off a piece and smell it. If it smells foul or very pungent, bitter, or harsh, discard it. Rub some of the plant and its juices on the inside of a wrist and wait 15 minutes or so. If any reaction occurs, discard it. Touch a small piece to the tip of your tongue. If it tastes nasty in any way, discard it. If you intend to boil it before eating, do so now. This is generally a good idea. After it's done, put a pinch of the plant in your mouth and chew it well, waiting for any reaction. If there is none, move on to the next step, which is swallowing it. Now wait eight hours without taking anything else but water by mouth. At the end of that time, if all is well, eat a teaspoon of the plant prepared the same way as the pinch was and swallow it. Wait another eight hours. If all is still well, eat half a cup of the plant (again, prepared the same way) and wait the final eight hours. At the end of this 24-hour period, if you have experienced no reaction, the plant is considered safe to eat.

It is highly advisable for you to become extremely familiar with the edible plants in the regions you frequent. Each time I move to a new region I quickly learn the flora of the area. It is easy to do with the right references and perhaps a

Coconut Palms

The fruit of the prickly pear cactus is sweet and plentiful.

local expert to drag you around and make you smart. When venturing into unfamiliar country, take along a pocket reference book .

Berries grow everywhere. A *general rule* to follow when dealing with berries is that about 75 percent of all white berries growing in North America are toxic to some degree, as are 50 percent of all red berries, and 25 percent of all black or blue berries. This is not a hard-and-fast rule, merely a general guideline. Berries are easy and fun to learn.

Mushrooms can also be used for food in a survival situation. I have seen articles and books that claim mushrooms must be avoided because they are hard to identify, which may result in poisoning, and that they have no nutritional value. This is false.

While it is true that some edible mushrooms have toxic lookalikes, many are easily identified and very common, and many do have nutritional value. The key is to become familiar with them or have a good mushroom book handy, and never eat one you are not 100 percent sure of. There are plenty of mushrooms out there that are excellent eating and almost impossible to misidentify. I have eaten mushrooms all over the world (wild ones, wise guy, not store-bought models) and never had a problem. And I am no expert on them, either.

When it comes to animals, it's just about anything goes. You can eat nearly every creature you can catch, though some will be better eating than others. And if you can't eat it, you can probably use it for bait in a trap or snare. Can you eat a porcupine? Yep. Can you eat a skunk? Yep. Can you eat a crocodile? Yep. Can he eat you? Yep, and there's one of the drawbacks. Like the saying goes, "Sometimes they say that you eat the bear, and sometimes the bear eats you." Common sense is the key.

Which is better, hunting or setting traps and snares? Careful. This is a trick question.

The answer is neither, for it depends entirely on the circumstances you find yourself in. While in the actual act of

The gray squirrel is a sucker for the squirrel pole approach.

wayfinding you can hunt as you go. While encamped for the night, you can set traps and snares before you turn in for the evening. They will do the hunting for you while you sleep. In the morning you can check your sets and reap the benefits of your crafty, woodswise ways.

Is it better to go after large game or small game? That depends on what is available. Caribou may be your most likely target (for hunting and snares) on the tundra, but in the bayous of Louisiana you should be after small game such as birds and fish. You make the call.

Generally speaking, small game isn't as smart as large game, and that makes them easier to catch. A squirrel borders on mental deficiency when compared to an elk. A sunfish is as dumb as a rock when compared to a bonefish. Get the idea? And the small game is often

Squirrel Pole

much more plentiful than large, though I admit that this isn't always the case. Rabbits and hares are easy prey for traps and snares, and many fish are downright stupid. Suckers, carp, catfish, sunfish, and other less intellectual fish are easy pickins. Suckers and catfish are mighty fine tasting, too.

Hunting takes much less practice, for the most part, than traps and snares, though I suspect that hunters who have never tried to trap or snare an animal would disagree. When you set a snare, rub ashes or conifer resin on the wire to mask the human scent, or carry a bottle of commercial scent mask. Rig your set where there is obvious sign of an animal, such as along trails and runs, and set it for one species of creature. General purpose snares do not fare nearly so well as species-specific snares. Set the snare

Fixed-Trail Snare

and get away from it. Check it twice a day or so, unless it is of a design that requires you to be nearby, such as an Ojibwa bird snare.

Some final thoughts on food and water procurement:

(1) Purify all water, no matter where you got it. *All water*. No exceptions. This can be done chemically (halazone, iodine, bleach) or by boiling. Never think that clarity means purity; it doesn't. Natural contaminants such as *Campylobacter jejuni* and *Giardia lamblia* are common. If either one gets a hold of your insides, stand by.

(2) Don't be squeamish about eating insects, slugs, worms, frogs, and other items not normally associated with run-of-the-mill restaurants in this country.

(3) Use every part of every animal you kill. Nothing should be wasted when surviving.

SHELTERS

Whether you are wayfinding with your shelter on your back, or you intend to let nature provide for you, you are going to have to find a place for your nightly home. As any realtor will tell you, location means everything.

The best Kelty tent on the market will only be of limited use to you unless you select the right spot to pitch it. The same is true of building a shelter from scratch. The wrong shelter site could mean anything from minor discomfort to death and everything in between.

When selecting a place for the night, take in the big picture. Think about your selection in a worst-case scenario. Murphy's Law applies well when it comes to shelter sites. Could that dry arroyo that hasn't seen so much as a drop of water in the last two months suddenly come to life, even if you can't see, hear, or feel rain anywhere in the vicinity? In a heartbeat! Flash floods are remarkably common in the desert. A rainstorm in the distant high country might never be detected by you, and if you are so foolish as to make camp in or beside an arroyo, you could pay with your life.

Flash floods take lives every year in America, and the Southwest is particularly susceptible.

What about land and mudslides? California is notorious for these killers. You can look at a piece of terrain and know instantly if it has a proclivity for slides. Trees, brush, and rocks strewn about the slope are clear indicators.

Never build too close to a water source in the spring, summer, or early autumn. The insects that live around water will make your life a living hell.

The lee side of a hill or mountain may be much drier than the windward side. In valleys, select a site about two-thirds of the way up the slope in the winter. Cold air sinks into the valley floor, making the lower areas quite a bit colder.

Look for natural shelters such as rock overhangs (caves are pretty rare in most parts of the country), blowdowns, and hollow logs. Of course, there may be something already living therein, so clear it out before you crawl in. Bats, bobcats, spiders, snakes, owls, ogres, armadillos, ants, and a plethora of other creatures all make their homes in what nature provides for them. Some don't take kindly to being evicted, either, so use caution.

Select a site that faces south or east, as these warm faster in the morning.

Watch for animal trails nearby. Don't build a shelter in the middle of a moose trail. I know of one wilderness survival student who did this, and he got a rude surprise in the middle of the night—namely about 1,000 pounds of moose trashing the shelter he was in.

Hollow Log

Lean-To

One-Pole A-Frame

When you do set up your shelter, the weather is your prime consideration. Always build as if you were going to face some serious stuff that night. Thatching must be tight and layered. Boughs and limbs must be strong and lashed well.

Face the smallest surface into the wind. Don't take shortcuts.

Finally, stow all your gear in the shelter if at all possible. Wildlife love to run off with or destroy gear. Also, never leave food of any kind lying out. (In bear country, hang foodstuffs between two limbs high enough off the ground that they can't get at them.) Keep the area clean, and don't eat right in front of your shelter, as the crumbs you drop will attract insects, rodents, and who knows what else.

I'm going to break it off here as far as survival goes. Let's move on to the weather.

CHAPTER NINE

WEATHER OR NOT

A s I peck away at my word processor's keyboard, the TV is yakking in the living room about the Great Flood of '93. The news magazines lying strewn about the den are filled with facts and figures concerning this epic flood, and both the mediums say that there is no end in sight. In fact, they say that it is going to get worse before it even thinks about getting better.

Hurricane Andrew trashed southern Florida a short while back, and the region has yet to recover. As with the Midwest, people are pretty much left to fend for themselves until the government can get some help to them.

North Carolina was stomped in the spring of '93 by a ferocious blizzard the likes of which no one has seen in these parts in decades.

And as I write, the entire eastern seaboard is experiencing a heat wave that is killing people left and right. The heat index is currently 115°F.

That's just in America, where we have homes to protect us from the ravages of nature's weather whims. But we see here that our homes are of limited or no use against nature when she gets a burr under her saddle. Imagine what such weather patterns would do to the wilderness wayfinder who suddenly finds himself fight-

Elevation can make a big difference in weather, water availability, and other wayfinding and survival considerations.

ing for his life far from the pleasant amenities of civilization as we know it.

Man has been trying to accurately predict the weather for thousands of years. He has come far, too. His satellites whizzing around in orbit see and tell all, or at least take a good shot at it. We see hurricanes forming off the western coast of Africa as the hot air masses over the Sahara clash with the moisture of the Atlantic, then move westward toward the peaceful Caribbean. But the wilderness traveler doesn't have monitors with him to check in with the Weather Channel every 30 minutes. He doesn't have the daily newspaper telling him what is probably going to happen over the next day or so. All he has are his senses and his brain.

And that is often all he needs.

NATURE'S CLUES

Nature often provides the observant wayfinder with

subtle clues as to what's in store for the region as far as weather goes. The stars, animals, plants, atmospheric colors and other signs, wind direction, and cloud types all can tell us what is about to happen.

Yesterday I was watching two bobwhite quail in my backyard taking a pleasant dirt bath. They threshed out a shallow depression beside the sweetgum and white oak and went to it. Dirt was flying everywhere, and they really seemed to enjoy what they were doing. I knew that they were dusting primarily to keep lice and other vermin at bay, but for some reason birds often take dirt baths when rain is approaching. The South had been experiencing a horrendous drought, and I hoped the birds were right and that it would rain soon. Less than six hours later, it poured.

Right after the bobwhites finished their dirt bath, I walked into the woods out back looking for other signs of inclement weather approaching. The first thing I noticed about the usually cacophonous woods was the silence. The cardinals, eastern bluebirds, Carolina chickadees, woodpeckers, and other birds were strangely quiet. A breeze picked up from the southeast. The deerflies were out in force more so than usual, another indicator. All these signs led me to believe that the bobwhites were right; rain was on the way.

There are other signs, too. When birds that normally fly at a certain height decide to fly lower, rain is coming. The thinner air caused by a low-pressure zone makes it harder for the birds to fly, so they don't fly so high or as long. Spiders can tell, too. If a walk in the woods reveals that they are not spinning webs, then they know that rain is not far off. Spiders know that rain falling on their webs has a tendency to break them. If you come across a line of ants not carrying food particles, rain is likely.

An increase in humidity is often associated with thunderstorms. Humidity affects plants, whose fragrance increases with the humidity. If your nose seems unusually sensitive to the aroma of plants and their flowers, rain is probably nearby.

The well-known saying, "Red sky at night, sailors delight. Red sky at morning, sailors take warning," has a lot of truth in it. It has to do with dust and dirt particles being suspended in the air by wind. Winds in the United States are primarily westerly. If the sky is reddish at sunset, then there is dust and dirt in the air. That air is dry, meaning good weather approaching from the west. If the morning sky is red, it simply means that the dry air has passed by us. Does this guarantee rain soon? No, but it does increase the chances of rain, since dry weather just went by.

Cirrus clouds, those high, wispy clouds that run ahead of warm fronts and rain showers, are made of ice crystals. They are the cause of sun and moon "dogs," those weird rings that encircle these heavenly bodies. As the front gets closer, the rings widen. Rain can be expected well within a day.

I was told as a boy that if a star appeared to have a bluish tinge, it was a cold star. If it was red, it was a hot star. If it twinkled, it was a star, but if it glowed, it was a planet. All this was bum scoop. Stars appearing blue do so because humid air sucks up red in the spectrum, leaving the stars blue. Humid air means rain is likely on the way. Stars twinkle because of upper atmosphere winds, i.e., the jetstream is over you.

Where I was raised in Maine, small dairies and farms were commonplace. When the cows were lying down together in mid-day, rain usually showed up soon thereafter. We burned plenty of wood in the fall and winter, and if we wanted to know if it was going to snow soon, we'd check the chimney. If the smoke was ascending and then suddenly dispersing and staying low just above the trees, snow was certain.

TERRAIN EFFECTS ON WEATHER

Ever been to Buffalo, New York, in the winter? No? Well, if you go, bring a shovel. Buffalo has some of the most horrendous snows in the United States. Why? The snow is lake-effect snow coming off Lake Erie. The Great Lakes are notorious for whipping up snowstorms that produce whiteout conditions and dumps astounding amounts of snow in a very short time. Buffalo just happens to be in the perfect spot for these snows, at the northeast corner of the lake. Such storms have a chance to really get cranking as they come barreling across the Great Plains and then hit the moisture over the Great Lakes.

The point here is that terrain can have drastic effects on local weather. I once saw a squall come down off of Ragged Mountain above the Maine seaport village of Rockport and descend right onto the harbor. The devastation it visited upon the tiny, picturesque harbor was startling. Schooner masts were toppled, boats capsized, and general pandemonium ensued. It lasted only a few minutes, but that was all it took to trash the place. The maniacal tempest then fled the scene with the same dispatch with which it arrived. I doubt if the tourists who were visiting the harbor will ever forget that little demonstration.

Mountain ranges, even single mountains and peaks, can have great effect on the local weather. The students at the U.S. Navy Survival School often commented on the weather, and how fast and drastically it changed, sometimes several times each day. I once saw it snow on July 4th. It's nothing to have a beautiful, sunny day at one end of the property (a 10,000 acre or so tract) and have a blizzard at the other end. The Redington Pond Range does this, and this is the case with many such ranges.

Steve ("Skeet") King, my childhood friend and accomplice who now lives in Colorado Springs, showed me how the Front Range behind his house can create wondrous thunderstorms at the proverbial drop of a hat. We were sitting on his deck overlooking a wildlife corridor that is his backyard, the warm spring air decorated with the delicate aroma of the antelope steaks his wife, Kathy, was fixing up, when he pointed to a hideous mass of absolutely black clouds streaking down the mountains

Water remains in an arroyo after a flash flood.

toward us. We dashed inside just before it hit. The electrical display and torrents of wind-whipped rain that drenched the area were most impressive, and then it was gone, on its way out over the Great Plains that start a few miles east of his home.

Elevation is another important ingredient in local weather. There is hardly ever a bad snowstorm at Steve's house, but ascend a couple of thousand feet and whoa! It's a whole different story. Snow everywhere and plenty of it.

A BOLT FROM THE BLUE

Lightning is clearly the most serious sudden weather hazard to wilderness travelers, even though the odds of your being struck sometime during your life are astronomical. Nevertheless, lightning nails a slew of people every year in this country. It travels at speeds of up to 100,000 miles per second and pulses at 55,000°F at the height of the most powerful bursts. Not something to play around with, eh?

According to the American Red Cross and National Weather Service, 300 or so people die from lightning strikes every year in this country, with another 700 being struck but not killed.

The most graphic danger lies in the direct hit, where the lightning has nothing to slow it down or mellow its power; it hits the victim dead-on. Next to this is the direct transmission, where something is between the bolt and the victim, such as an antenna. Then there is the "splash," where people are struck by lightning as it overflows from the first object it hit. Ground current is very common. The bolt hits a tree or other object, flows into the ground, and spreads out. You can be injured by the shock wave created by the burst even though the current never reaches you. It can break bones, shatter eardrums, and knock you clean out.

I am not going to bore you with advice on how to avoid lightning strikes. You know that already. Just use caution and take steps to avoid the problem. Remember that lightning can reach out and get you even if you are not beneath a thunderhead.

I really can't see turning this into a meteorology handbook. If you want to learn more about the weather, watch the Weather Channel or buy a book on it. I'll leave you with one piece of advice on the weather: as someone who spends time out of doors and off the beaten track, you had better know how to handle weather extremes in a moment's notice. The weather will slay you if you ignore or underestimate it.

CHAPTER TEN

THE GREAT ALONE

W ell, it has been quite a journey. We've been just about everywhere, I'd say, and the trek has been enlightening, challenging, and spirited. We have come to know many things in these pages, which I hope you will not soon forget (you won't, if I have done my job). I've bent your ear a bit in the process, but I think the goal has indeed been achieved, that being to teach you every possible aspect about wilderness wayfinding.

By now you realize that wayfinding is much, much more than using a map and compass to run an azimuth. It involves skills, attributes, and a train of thought that goes far beyond getting from here to there. Wayfinding is an ancient skill developed and honed by our distant ancestors. I invented none of the skills discussed herein. No one alive did. What I have done is put all these skills in one text for the first time, and I have tried to do so in a way that was informative, fun, and interesting.

Is there one key skill above all others that will keep you on the right path? Yes, there is. It is called confidence. If you are confident in your map, compass, knowledge of nature and terrain, and your own wayfinding skills, you won't go wrong very often. From time to time you will still get turned around, but that is part of the fun! Don't be afraid to guesstimate. Take a chance. If it works, fine. If it doesn't, better luck next time. Be bold. Look around you. What do you see? Can you see it on the map? Does your compass work? If it doesn't or you don't have one, it doesn't matter. You can always tell direction. Go for it.

Survival skills are extremely important to the wilderness wayfinder. Develop these and your confidence will soar.

Although North America's population of humans is growing at an outrageous rate, there are still plenty of wild places out there to lose yourself in. Seek them out. Take a friend if you like, or go it alone. There is no feeling like that you experience when you are absolutely alone in a wild place. A place you arrived at by deduction, skill, and self-confidence. This is Service's Great Alone, and there is nothing like it. Whether you are standing atop an escarpment on the Dark Continent, peering down onto the Ucayali from South America's Cordillera Oriental, or just taking in the magnificence of the Lewis and Clark Range, you will come to know the feeling of wilderness.

Perhaps our paths will cross one day in The Great Alone.